In her book, *Pilgrim Psalms*, Kathy McReynolds reflects upon the Psalms to teach us how to be spiritual pilgrims – genuine seekers after Christ. In a clear, conversational, and interesting style, she offers sound and solid Scriptural advice to Christians of all ages. A beautifully-written study.

Denise George

All believers are pilgrims on a journey from a world of suffering and difficulty to the heavenly throne room of our glorious Savior. Kathy McReynolds has given us more than "bread crumbs" to follow along the challenging path often strewn with discontentment and overgrown with discouragement. Believers are equipped with the light of Scripture beautifully flowing through these *Pilgrim Psalms*, which, together with the author's inspirational insights, comprise the heart of this volume, and are transferred to our hearts by the Holy Spirit.

Dorothy Kelley Patterson

This book is a helpful academic look at the psalms for those whose faith has become stagnant or unexciting.

Fiona Castle

THE PILGRIM PSALMS

A Sacred Journey to revitalize your life

Kathy McReynolds

CHRISTIAN FOCUS

To My Wonderful Husband, Mike
and
To My Three Beautiful Children, Jessica, Moriah, and Jeremiah
May We All Continue To Be The Lord's Pilgrims
"One Love, One God, One Way"
(KJ52)

Copyright © Kathy McReynolds 2006

ISBN 1-85792-927-0 (10)
ISBN 987-1-85792-927-0 (13)

10 9 8 7 6 5 4 3 2 1

Printed in 2006
by
Christian Focus Publications, Geanies House,
Fearn, Ross-shire, IV20 1TW, Scotland

www.christianfocus.com

Cover design by Alister MacInnes (info@moose77.com)

Printed and bound by Bercker, Germany.

CONTENTS

INTRODUCTION

~~~~~~~~~~~~~~~~~~~~~~~~~~~~

Why This Book?

The alarm went off at 5:30 a.m. as usual. But I was not in my usual mood. Most mornings I wake up at 5:30 a.m. with a sense of excitement and anticipation because it is my time with the Lord. For one blessed hour I have the opportunity to meditate on God's Word and lay my requests at his throne of grace, without interruption. It is usually such a refreshing and uplifting experience. But this particular morning, my heart just was not in it. Something was not right, but I could not put my finger on it.

What I mean is that I am usually in some kind of crisis when I feel this way. But things could not have been better. I felt I was "right" with the Lord. My family was healthy, happy, and growing spiritually. I was finishing up my doctoral work at USC and teaching part-time at Biola University in La Mirada, California. Our food distribution ministry in Watts was thriving. What was the problem?

Well, I got my coffee and opened my Bible. I happened to be in the Book of Psalms that day, which is always a good thing when you are feeling a little moody! As I was reading along in Psalm 120, the following words leapt out at me: "Woe to me that I dwell in Meshech, that I live among the tents of Kedar!" (Ps. 120:5) I thought to myself, "That's it! That's what is wrong with me! I am dwelling in a place that is far from the Lord!"

I know at first glance it may be hard to believe that I could receive that kind of revelation from such a seemingly strange verse. However, the writer of Psalm 120 is conveying that very message. He is physically in a place that is far from the Lord and he is expressing his utter discontentment with his situation. Well, that spoke volumes to me.

My problem was that, from a spiritual standpoint, discontentment had set in. Yes, on the outside, I seemed to have it all together. I was consistently involved in the spiritual disciplines: studying the Bible, praying, involved in ministry, and attending church regularly. But, still, in my heart, I got off track. How did it happen? I believe I became so content with my earthly situation that my spiritual life also became "content."

Without even realizing it, I stopped growing in Christ. I stopped yearning for his presence. I stopped searching for his will. Needless to say, if you are a true believer, this kind of spiritual stagnation will always bring about discontentment. Now, spiritual stagnation happens quite subtly, especially when you are doing the things you are supposed to do as a Christian. But the effects are still the same: something will not be right with you, even when everything apparently is.

As I continued to read through the pilgrim psalms (Ps. 120-134), I had another revelation, so to speak. In the historical context, these psalms were apparently read and/or sung as the Israelites ascended to Jerusalem (since Jerusalem is on a high place) to celebrate the appointed feasts: the Feast of Unleavened Bread, the Feast of Firstfruits, and the Feast of Tabernacles (Ex. 23:15-16). Psalms 122-134 may have been read in Jerusalem, possibly even ascending up the steps to the Temple itself.

With this in mind, it came to me that these pilgrim psalms may actually have a wider and more obvious value applied today than in their original setting. Under the Old Covenant, these psalms were used a few times each year when the Israelites were going up to Jerusalem, where the glorious presence of the Lord resided, for a festal occasion. Today, both our individual bodies (1 Cor. 6:19) and the church (1 Cor. 3:16) are the "temple of the Holy Spirit." So, rather than being used annually, as they were in their original setting, the pilgrim psalms can be used daily. Because of the special nature of these psalms, they have timeless value.

Well, I immediately began to apply these insights to my situation. I began to reflect daily on these wonderful little psalms and, before long, I found myself on a journey — a sacred one — into the Lord's presence. I began to understand in a new and fresh way that God is calling me to be a *pilgrim*. To be the Lord's pilgrim is to be someone who journeys not just to any place, but to *the* sacred place — to the temple where the glorious Lord resides. The pilgrim psalms represent the pilgrimage we all must take to "ascend" into the Lord's presence. As I said before, because we are now the temple of the Holy Spirit, this pilgrimage involves the inner life. It means that we must seek the One who indwells us.

When we seek to know God in this way, when we seek to integrate our faith with knowledge and action, we begin our journey into the Lord's presence. The purpose of this book is to help you to begin this sacred journey. By reflecting on the various themes woven through the pilgrim psalms we will begin to discern the steps that we must take to ascend into the presence of the One who indwells us. Now, this is *not* a formula guaranteed to bring about the desired results if it is followed in a precise way. Rather, it is simply a journey that involves certain spiritual disciplines that are essentially the same for all of us. But for each of us, the journey is always different. We are all unique, and though we are all destined to the same place, the pilgrimage we make is quite unique in many aspects.

Therefore, a set formula simply could never suffice.

Whenever I discuss this journey with some of my believing friends, I usually get comments like the following: I am a very busy person. How can I take the time to pursue this journey? My family, church, career and community all expect so much from me. I am up at 6 a.m. and it is non-stop as soon as my feet hit the floor. I wake the children, get them dressed, fed, and off to school. I clean the breakfast mess and go to work. After work, I stop by the grocery store. I come home and make dinner, clean the mess, bathe the children, and put them to bed. Then I make lunches, and, finally, I fall exhausted into my bed. As if this were not enough, someone like you tells me that if I want the spiritual contentment I long for, I must take this journey!

Well, that is exactly what I am saying! Look, I am just like you. I know the hustle and bustle of daily life. I know what it is to be tired and stressed. And, like you, I also know spiritual discontentment. I have experienced it long enough to know that I do not want to live my life under its cloud. I have also learned that coming to this point in my life was the best thing that ever happened to me. Discontentment brought me to that place where I was ready to become the Lord's pilgrim again.

Unlike any other group of psalms, the pilgrim psalms speak to our common longings and experiences. Consider again that seemingly strange verse from Psalm 120, "Woe to me that I dwell in Meshech, that I live among the tents of Kedar!" This psalmist is clearly in distress. He lives among a people who do not know his God. In the country in which he was living, he was probably quite well off materially but, still, there was something amiss. He was clearly unsettled and motivated to seek change.

Like the psalmist, our pilgrimage into the Lord's presence begins with the experience of discontentment and with a desire for change. If you are discontent with your spiritual life and motivated to move on, then this book will probably prove to be a great source of encouragement to you. However, a steadfast heart and mind is needed in order to hear and to act on the truth revealed in these psalms. The reason for this is that obstacles are bound to cross our path.

The Pilgrim's Stumbling Stones

As you may know, a journey to any place can sometimes be filled with obstacles. There may be flight delays or a car that breaks down. Someone may become ill or loose a plane ticket. Any number of things may occur to delay a person's arrival at a certain destination. In the same way, as pilgrims on a spiritual journey, our path can become riddled with stumbling stones. I have already mentioned how our hectic schedules can short-circuit our progress. In this book we will focus not only on this "stone" but also on the intellectual and emotional stones that can block our way.

Intellectual blocks may include a lack of confidence. Sometimes we can tell ourselves things like, "I'm not theologically educated enough to really understand Scripture." This can become a huge stumbling stone! But the truth is that *all* believers can learn to be confident in the knowledge of Scripture. We can all learn to think through the implications and applications of God's word. It is a matter of the will to do so.

Sometimes we refuse Scripture's instruction because we think we know enough to get us through our trials. During these times an examination of our motives is needed. Learning to discern whether our struggle is with spiritual darkness or with the pull of worldly values or with our own desires sometimes takes great effort. During these times it is also important to realize that our intellect plays an enormous role in these battles.

Emotional blocks can include a lack of desire for God's presence. This can happen when emotions are the sole basis of our relationship with God. We short-circuit our ability to grow spiritually because we only desire God when we feel good. An inability to express our emotions properly can also stifle our journey. This difficulty to express our emotions may spring from childhood experiences, from poor choices, or from fear of taking risks. As overwhelming as these emotional stones can be, they nevertheless can be overcome *if* there is a will to do so.

Only a willing and humble heart-- a heart that is open to the Lord's mysterious ways-- can enable us to overcome these seemingly insurmountable stumbling stones. On the more practical side, what is also needed for the journey are some "tools" for the study of psalms.

Practical Tools for the Study of Psalms

There are several principles involved in reading, applying, and understanding the psalms. As our journey unfolds, we will gain further insight into these principles. But at the outset, we want to mention a few things here. In order to unlock the door to the deepest treasures in the pilgrim psalms, three principles need to be kept in mind: 1) each individual psalm should be read completely; 2) each individual verse should be interpreted in light of the whole psalm; 3) the author's intent in the psalm must be discerned *before* we apply the psalm to our lives.

The other issue of interpretation worth mentioning here is the use of poetic repetition. The repetition of words and thoughts stated in slightly different ways is common in the psalms. Frequently this poetic language paints word pictures by comparing similar and dissimilar objects to emphasize a point.[1] When thoughts, words or phrases are repeated or reworded, the thought is intended for further meditation. These repetitions emphasize important themes within the psalm. It is truly a blessing that spiritual growth consists of many daily steps and small decisions because we can build continuously on each small success. But we may also need to stretch ourselves in faithful response to the Lord's leading. Yes, we can make this pilgrimage into the Lord's presence. The pilgrim psalms provide us with some wonderful metaphors and illustrations of this sacred journey. The willing heart may stumble, but the Lord of heaven has promised that he will lead his faithful followers to his holy hill.

Our pilgrimage will begin with a closer look at what it means to be the Lord's pilgrim. Then, by reflecting and meditating on the pilgrim psalms, we will first examine the ways in which discontentment prompts our pilgrimage

(Ps. 120). Then we will explore God's role in providing for the journey (Ps. 121-125) and how our dependence on him leads to a deeper revelation of where true blessings come from (Ps. 126-129). We will then discuss in light of God's provisions and blessings what our responses to him ought to be; namely, confession, humility, and consistent meditation on his promises (Ps. 130-132). These disciplines prepare us to metaphorically draw near to the Temple in Zion, where the glorious Lord resides (Ps. 133-134). We will draw parallels between this sacred entrance into Zion and spiritual maturity. The implication is that the mature believer is a "worshiping" believer. By drawing practical applications from our pilgrimage to Zion, we will learn of ways to consistently abide in the holy presence of our Lord.

Notes
[1] For more on this see William W. Klein, Craig L. Blomberg, Robert L. Hubbard, *Introduction to Biblical Interpretation*, Chapter 7 (Dallas: Word, 1993), p. 245.

ONE

~~~~~~

The Lord's Pilgrim

Tommy's Story

When I was a graduate student at the University of Southern California, I took a class on problems in medical and biomedical ethics. The class requirements were interesting and exciting. Each week we had to visit a unit either in the general hospital, the women's hospital, or the children's hospital. These units included every major specialty from neonatology to gerontology. In these contexts we learned about the kinds of traumas and illnesses each unit treated and about the treatments that were required for particular patients. Then we were presented with certain ethical dilemmas that each unit faced on an almost daily basis, and we were asked to try to come up with solutions.

Our week at the children's hospital was one of the most unique and moving experiences of the entire semester. In this setting we were told not to take notes or to ask questions or to make ethical decisions. We were simply supposed to sit down and listen to a mother describe her experience with her very ill son.[1] When Tommy was born, he appeared to be healthy and normal. But, by his first birthday, it became apparent that there may be a problem. He could not sit up by himself and he could not use his hands and feet in the way that most one-year-old children could.

His mother took him to his pediatrician and he tried to assure her that Tommy was "just a little slow." All of his tests came back normal, so there was nothing really to worry about. Not long after this, Tommy developed a swallowing problem. Every time he tried to eat, he would choke until he vomited. Then he developed vision problems and his co-ordination was getting worse. The physicians ran numerous tests and evaluations. In fact, they ran so many tests that one particular day the charges amounted to over $15,000! But there were still no conclusive answers. This went on for years, and Tommy's condition continued to worsen.

When Tommy was about five years of age, his mother became pregnant with her second child. Tragically, when she was nine months pregnant and about to give birth, the baby died in utero. She became pregnant again and the same thing happened, only this time she was about six months pregnant. As a result of these terrible losses, Tommy's mother and father underwent some genetic testing to try to determine what caused them. It was discovered that both of them carried a recessive gene which was responsible for passing on to their children a rare metabolic disorder. Every child they would ever conceive would have this devastating disorder.

Finally, they understood what was wrong with Tommy. There was no cure for this disease, and it would eventually take his life if a cure was not found. But doctors believed they could at least give Tommy a decent quality of life with certain treatments. Tommy did respond well to some treatments and he actually had some good days when he was able to eat and drink and enjoy his friends and family. Tommy's parents adopted two older children, who eventually fell in love with him. He did struggle terribly at times with his disease, but at least he knew he was loved.

According to his mother, Tommy had such a sweet spirit about him. He was tender and caring and genuinely seemed happy. He was able to learn and to read in a limited capacity and he seemed to be interested in so many things. However, there was one thing that consistently puzzled his mother. Tommy never seemed to be truly content. He would tell her on occasion that he was not supposed to be here. He was supposed to be somewhere else and that he was looking forward to that day when he would be where he was supposed to be. She did not completely understand what he meant and sometimes it scared her.

When Tommy was about nine years of age, he developed kidney and lung problems as part of the progression of his disease. He was in and out of the hospital and, on several occasions, he was near death. The doctors told his family there was nothing more that they could do for him. But his parents still insisted on intubating him when he could not breathe on his own. They were not yet ready to give up the fight for their son's life.

Finally, on one particular day, while Tommy lay there on the hospital bed, his mother noticed that he appeared so peaceful. His mother then looked deeply into his eyes and asked him a question, "Tommy, do you want to fight?" "I am not supposed to be here," replied Tommy. "Do you want to go home?" his mother asked. "Yes," said Tommy. Then his mother, with tears in her eyes, made an agonizing decision. She released him. "Go home, my son," she said, "and I will see you soon." Tommy died an hour later. The peace and tranquility Tommy's mother saw on her son's face when he died helped her to finally understand what he meant when he continually said that he was not supposed to be here. He was a pilgrim, the Lord's pilgrim, sent here for a little while to bless those around him, and then to go to his true home in heaven.

Called to Wander

Though Tommy's story is extremely sad and tragic, it vividly illustrates what it means to be the Lord's pilgrim. In the worldly sense, a pilgrim is a person who journeys, especially long distances, to some sacred place as an act of religious devotion. The *Lord's* pilgrim, in contrast, journeys ultimately to The Sacred Place, where God himself dwells, as his or her act of religious devotion. This is what Tommy did.

Also, in the worldly sense, a pilgrim is a traveler or wanderer, especially in a foreign place. A pilgrim in this sense could very well settle down in a particular foreign place and make it his or her home. The *Lord's* pilgrim, however, is someone who could never be truly content in this world. It was C.S. Lewis who said that if we find in ourselves a desire that this world cannot satisfy, then we must be meant for another world. And this is exactly what Tommy realized in his dire circumstances. From the time he could talk, Tommy expressed his discontentment with this world. He never truly felt at home here. This discontentment was not a result of his disease-stricken body, but of something that was deeply rooted in his spirit.

There are many examples in Scripture of people whom the Lord called to wander. In the Old Testament, God spoke to Abraham while he was still living in Mesopotamia and said:

> Leave your country, your people and your father's household and go to the land I will show you. I will make you into a great nation and I will bless you. I will make your name great, and you will be a blessing (Gen. 12:1-2).

God sent Abraham to the land of Canaan – the place where He himself would ultimately dwell – so that he could be with the nation that he would create from the loins of Abraham. Once they were called, God's people were never truly content anywhere outside the Promised Land. Jacob, son of Abraham, went to live for twenty years in Paddan Aram, his mother's homeland. But he longed for Caanan, and God ultimately brought him back to the land he promised to his father, Abraham. (Gen. 31–35).

Joseph, son of Jacob, was sent to Egypt as a slave. When famine broke out in Canaan, Jacob and his entire family went to live in Egypt. As the familiar story goes, Jacob's descendants, the Israelites, were enslaved there in Egypt, and Moses, by the power of God, delivered them and brought them to Mount Horeb, where God was waiting for them (Ex. 1–12). There they found contentment.

Because of their sin Israel wandered in the desert for forty years. But Joshua brought the second generation of Israelites into Canaan, where they lived until the time of the Assyrian (722 BC) and Babylonian (586 BC) exiles (Joshua, Judges, 1 and 2 Samuel, 1 and 2 Kings). In these cases, clearly the Israelites' sin, and not God's purposive will, was the cause of their wanderings. But the point is that the Israelites, once they were called, were never content anywhere outside the Promised Land. Consider Psalm 137:

> By the rivers of Babylon we sat and wept
>   when we remembered Zion.
> There on the poplars we hung our harps,

for there our captors asked us for songs,
our tormentors demanded songs of joy; they said,
"Sing us one of the songs of Zion!"

How can we sing the songs of the Lord
in a foreign land?
If I forget you, O Jerusalem, may my right hand forget
its skill.
May my tongue cling to the roof of my mouth
if I do not remember you, if I do not consider Jerusalem
my highest joy.

(Ps. 137:1-6)

Why Jerusalem? It is because Jerusalem is the place where the God of heaven dwells on earth. His Temple was the center of all activity in Jerusalem, and God called his people to dwell with him there, in the heart of the land which he promised to Abraham, Isaac, and Jacob, their forefathers. Therefore, the Israelites became his pilgrims. This calling, by necessity, made them *strangers* in this world. In Psalm 119, the writer says, "I am a stranger on earth; do not hide your commands from me" (v. 19).

In the same way, the pilgrim psalms beautifully illustrate that "stranger mentality," that longing of the Israelites to be in that sacred place where God dwells. And, as I said in the Introduction, the pilgrim psalms apply to believers today because we, too, have been called to be the Lord's pilgrims.

A Heavenly Destination

When Jesus was being questioned by the Jews about his ministry, he told them the following: "You are from below; I am from above. You are of this world; I am not of this world" (John 8:23). Later, when Jesus was on trial before Pilate, he said, "My kingdom is not of this world. If it were, my servants would fight to prevent my arrest by the Jews. But now my kingdom is from another place" (John 18:36).

The apostles carried this same message throughout their ministry and encouraged the church to be true to their heavenly calling. Paul told the Philippian church, for example, that "our citizenship is in heaven. And we eagerly await a Savior from there, the Lord Jesus Christ, who, by the power that enables him to bring everything under his control, will transform our lowly bodies so that they will be like his glorious body" (Phil. 3:20-21).

In his first epistle, the Apostle Peter called believers "strangers in the world" and gave them this encouragement: "Dear friends, I urge you as aliens and strangers in the world, to abstain from sinful desires, which war against your soul. Live such good lives among the pagans that, though they accuse you of doing wrong, they may see your good deeds and glorify God on the day he visits us" (1 Pet. 2:11-12).

In Hebrews 11, the writer holds up many of the Old Testament saints and Jesus himself as shining examples who model for us the "pilgrim" mindset that should characterize every New Testament believer. Abel offered God a better sacrifice than Cain, showing forth his heavenly focus (v. 4). Enoch so pleased God in his earthly life that he was spared the experience of bodily death (v. 5). Though he had never experienced a flood, Noah, in holy fear, built an ark. His obedience saved the human race (v. 7).

I have already mentioned Abraham and the significance of his calling. But in Hebrews 11, his "pilgrim" status is emphasized in order to encourage the early Jewish Christians. He went and made his home in a foreign land because "he was looking forward to the city with foundations whose architect and builder is God" (v. 10). The visionary and humble leader Moses "chose to be mistreated along with the people of God rather than to enjoy the pleasures of sin for a short time. He regarded disgrace for the sake of Christ as of greater value than the treasures of Egypt" (vv. 25-26a). Why? It was because he was looking ahead to his reward. This is the true pilgrim mindset.

So, the Lord's pilgrim is one who ultimately journeys to The Heavenly Place, where God dwells, and not to a holy shrine or relic, which is only a mere representation of a spiritual reality. The Lord's pilgrim is also a wanderer in a foreign place, one who could never find true contentment in this world. Tommy and the Old and New Testament saints encourage us to stay true to our pilgrim calling. Church history is also filled with believers who described the Christian life as a pilgrimage. It is only when we truly see ourselves as we really are, the Lord's pilgrims, that the pilgrim psalms can begin to be meaningful to our lives.

Do you desire to live in the Lord's presence, fully and completely, without any hypocrisy? If you do, then at some level, you must have experienced that discontentment that Tommy spoke of. Come, let us turn to the pilgrim psalms and begin our journey with an intimate look at discontentment and the role it plays in our travels into the Lord's presence.

Notes

[1] The details of this case have been altered to protect the identity of those involved.

TWO

~~~~~~

"Woe to Me that I Dwell in Meshech!"
Discontentment: Psalm 120

We Citizens....

Perhaps the most overlooked aspect related to the quality of the Christian's spiritual life is the issue concerning citizenship. Now, when we think of citizenship, we typically think about the country in which we reside, voting, and taxes. For the Christian, however, citizenship means a bit more. The Apostle Paul, when writing to the Philippians, claimed that for believers in Jesus Christ, "our citizenship is in heaven" (Phil. 3:20).

The Apostle's point is that the Christian's ultimate home is heaven, in the presence of the Lord. However, as critical as this understanding is to Christian self-identity, it is easily misunderstood, simply because the context of Paul's discussion is not properly understood.

In order to address this critical issue concerning citizenship, a brief explanation of the circumstances of the believers in Philippi is necessary. After a major military victory in 42 BC, the Romans made Philippi a privileged colony. As such, it had rights such as tax exemption and legal status equivalent to the Italian cities. What that meant was, even though Philippi and its citizens were located in Macedonia, legally, it was as if they lived in Rome, with all the rights and privileges of that capital city.

That did not mean that their everyday life was much different from that of the people around them. Though the citizens of Philippi were proud of their status as a colony of Rome, their daily lives did not reflect their privileged status. In the same way, many of us are so bogged down with our daily lives that we are not living lives which reflect an immediate awareness of our heavenly citizenship. We may have a vague unease we cannot put our finger on or possibly even a gnawing sense of inner restlessness in our lives that won't go away. When faced with this kind of uncomfortable stirring down deep inside, we tend to emulate our unbelieving co-workers by burying ourselves deeper in our work or in countless other distractions. Instead, we need to understand that the Lord often uses such unsettled times to put us into positions in which we begin to yearn for a closer relationship with him.

A Season of Discontent

It takes no more than a slight glance to realize that the writer of Psalm 120 is uncomfortable in his current circumstances:

> In my trouble I cried to the Lord,
>   And he answered me.
> Deliver my soul, O Lord, from lying lips,
>   From a deceitful tongue.
> What shall be given to you, and what more
> shall be done to you,
>   You deceitful tongue?
> Sharp arrows of the warrior,
>   With the burning coals of the broom tree.
> Woe is me, for I sojourn in Meshech,
>   For I dwell among the tents of Kedar!
> Too long has my soul had its dwelling
>   With those who hate peace.
> I am for peace, but when I speak,
>   They are for war.

It is clear enough to grasp what he is wrestling with. On the other hand, it is not at all obvious where the psalmist is as he is doing that wrestling, or why his location would make any real difference. If we make our way through the psalm in the traditional sequential manner, it seems as if it is basically an anguished prayer (v. 1) of a sensitive soul who is deeply hurt by those who have either been lying to him or about him, as well as deceiving him (v. 2), seeking the Lord's vengeance on the perpetrators (vv. 3-4). But, then, that plea is mysteriously expanded by references to locations far off (v. 5) and the seemingly ominous mentions of war and peace (vv. 6-7).

When it is remembered, though, that this is the first of the Psalms of Ascent, the above first-glance understanding, frankly, is *under*whelming, to say the least. In other words, from the traditional perspective, it seems that there must be much more to it than that. But, if that is the case, how do we approach Psalm 120 in order to tap into its meaning and significance?

The "Shape" of the Psalm

Those of us who have grown up in the Western world, with the deeply-engrained legacy of Graeco-Roman inductive and deductive logic in our thinking and writing, we almost always look for clues to meaning in sequential order, often with an emphasis at the beginning (i.e., in the introduction) or at the end (i.e., in the conclusion). However, in many other parts of the world and for much of history, meaning has often been "constructed" in other shapes.

One of the most common types of literary structuring in the ancient world, especially in the biblical world of the Near East and Middle East, was parallelism. Parallelism is an elegant, and rhythmic, form of expression, and it has long been recognized that a verse or two of many psalms, which were Israel's hymnbook, employed either conventional (aba'b') or inverted (abb'a') parallel structures as an emphasis technique (i.e., micro-parallel structures). However, until relatively recently, apparently largely because of the "blinders" of the predominant

Western inductive-deductive logical format being read back onto the Bible, the possibility of longer passages, including entire psalms or complete biblical books, being developed as macro-parallel structures was flatly denied.

However, this perception has changed dramatically in recent decades as the evidence has begun to stack up to the point of being overwhelming.[1] In regard to the state of affairs related to the Book of Psalms, one of the very best of the recent commentaries on the Psalter, by Willem Van Gemeren,[2] employs this type of analysis in a rigorously thorough-going manner. We will refer consistently to Van Gemeren's excellent insights, though, on occasion, we will find it necessary to state that we think he has missed the correct emphasis and why, as well as some instances where his analysis is good, as far as it goes, but we do not think he probed far enough to capture the full range of what the author is seeking to communicate.

For example, Van Gemeren's understanding of the structure of Psalm 120 takes the following "shape":

A. Assurance of Answered Prayer (v. 1)
B. Prayer for Help (vv. 2-4)
B'. Expression of Desperation (v. 5)
A'. Longing for Peace (vv. 6-7)

The helpfulness of this structure is that it pairs the psalmist's assurance that the Lord will answer his prayers (v. 1) with his prayerful longing for peace (vv. 6-7), while reflecting that his sense of desperation (v. 5) is the prime motivating force of his prayer for help (vv. 2-4).

But, as helpful as this is in general, this basic structure is ultimately sketchy and does not capture the intended emphasis of the carefully nuanced parallels.

A more accurate, and much more detailed, understanding of the movement of Psalm 120 would be:

A. Crying out over trouble caused by deceivers (v. 1a)
B. God's answer to the psalmist's cry for help (v. 1b)
C. Requesting deliverance from liars and deceivers (v. 2)
D. Anticipating God's response to the deceitful tongue (v. 3)
D'. A figurative description of God's judgment of the deceitful tongue (v. 4)
C'. Dwelling in "Meshech" and "Kedar," among peace-haters (vv. 5-6)
B'. The psalmist's desire for "peace" (v. 7a)
A'. The deceivers' preference for "war" (v. 7b)

Here, the structural pairings make it clear, first, that the "trouble" the psalmist is wrestling with (v. 1a) is directly related to his enemies' war-like behavior (v. 7b), though it does not explain what that is. Secondly, in crying out to the Lord for help v. 1b), the psalmist is actually seeking "peace" (v. 7a). Thirdly, the liars and deceivers who are tormenting the life of the psalmist (v. 2) are said to be peace-haters (v. 6) who are found in "Meshech" and "Kedar" (v. 5). Finally, it is made clear that the Lord will judge the peace-haters and deceitful tongues in no uncertain terms (vv. 3-4).

As we begin our consideration of the spiritual ramifications of Psalm 120 for God's pilgrim, several crucial points have already been clarified by this structural understanding: 1) Spiritual warfare, as the term is generally used, i.e., in the unseen realm, is certainly not the only context for spiritual battles that believers face. Lying, deceitful people also provide very painful attacks with significant spiritual dimensions (vv. 1a, 7b); 2) Longing for deliverance from the "warring" of liars and deceivers can be a very significant spiritual step in the right direction, as long as the desired outcome is not simply peaceful coexistence with the world (vv. 1b-2, 5-7a); 3) Preparing to start the pilgrim's journey into the Lord's presence requires opening your eyes and, like the prodigal son (Luke 15:15-18), "coming to your senses" spiritually and admitting how far you are away from the Father and His desires for your life (vv. 1b-2, 5-7a); and 4) As we embark on our pilgrim's journey, we need not consider what will happen in regard to those who provided the torment that, providentially, the Lord used to get our attention and make our lives increasingly uncomfortable. God will take care of them (vv. 3-4).

Realizing the Only Way to Go is Up

Almost everyone who reads Psalm 120, and seeks to carefully understand it, will wonder what was the exact nature of the lying and deceitfulness (vv. 1-3) that the psalmist was struggling with. However, we have to assume that, if that information was required for the reader to derive the full spiritual profit intended, the writer (and the Lord) would have provided it. Given the nature of the pilgrim psalms, though, it seems quite likely that the references here in Psalm 120 are intentionally vague. In other words, what is intended by the psalmist to be communicated here is a timeless spiritual principle instead of a highly specific instance.

Think about it: if we had been told the exact kind of lies or deceiving that had come about and brought such distress into the psalmist's life, we would tend to reason that those were the only kinds of struggles that could legitimately provide the starting point for the spiritual pilgrim's journey. We would likely overlook many other troubling areas that equally well bring us to our knees before the Lord and convince and convict us that we are at a low point spiritually.

As intended here, almost any kind of trouble can be what gets our attention and begins the redirection of the path of our lives onto the ascending spiritual pathway. It is not necessary for us to hit rock bottom before we can look up. It is indeed very possible for the Lord to get our attention by means of anything we are struggling with in our lives without having to come to the point of "crashing and burning".

What makes the difference in a believer being able to face up to things without having to hit bottom? Very frequently, the issue is one of independence: wanting to be able to take care of our own problems, wanting to — whether it is ever admitted in the clear light of day or not — make it on our own. Spiritually, ultimately, that comes down to a root of pride that does not want to cry out to God for help; that does not want to admit that you cannot "get your act together" over this issue.

This is where Paul's perspective of "when I am weak, then I am strong" (2 Cor. 12:10) comes into play. Realizing and admitting how weak we are spiritually, then reaching out for the Lord, who is the source of all spiritual strength, is the mindset that allows the spiritual pilgrim to begin the journey of ascent without having to bottom out.

A Plea for Peace

There is a common tendency today to think of "peace" as simply and only the absence of hostility. If, however, we, shortsightedly, conclude that is the case in Psalm 120, we will settle for only a half truth at best. Yes, the psalmist yearned for deliverance from the viciousness of lies and the subtle betrayal of deceit by those around him. That is evident in the way the psalm begins. However, to think that is all the author had in mind displays no more insight than the person who looks at an iceberg and thinks that what is seen above the surface is the entirety of that massive floating chunk of ice. Instead, we must understand that the concept of "peace" in the Bible is one of those in which there is a great deal beneath "the tip of the iceberg."

The meaning of *Shalom*, the Hebrew word translated "peace", is very rich indeed. It actually speaks at least as much of "completeness, soundness and welfare" as it does of "peace."[3] When that is realized, it begins to dawn on the reader that the author of Psalm 120 is interested in a lot more than just relief from lying and deceit. Rather, it appears that it is the pain and frustration of his current

35

circumstances that have cause the psalmist to take stock of his life. The resulting self-diagnosis is a deep, and very troubling, sense of spiritual incompleteness.

This insight is drawn from two statements. The first has to do with the people the psalmist has been contending with: the external cause of his mounting discontent.

The second is a surprising self-characterization, one that is not easily discerned through English translations.

If we're not careful, we will tend to read the initial statement in the light of the ongoing explosive ethnic-political conflict in Israel: "Too long has my soul had its dwelling with those who hate peace" (Ps. 120:6). But, given the fuller understanding of *Shalom* discussed above, there appears to be much more in play here than individual or group conflict. The people in question don't just "hate" the possibility of resolution with the psalmist. They also don't want to have anything at all to do with the concept of spiritual completeness of life that is the essence of *Shalom*.

In stark contrast, in verse 7, instead of the translations "I am a man of peace" (NIV) or "I am for peace" (NASB), the Hebrew reads, literally, "I peace." Van Gemeren is close to capturing the power of this crisp assertion in saying: "In his whole being the psalmist longs for the establishment of peace."[4] To express what the author seems to be saying as a play on words: in his whole being, he longs to be whole in the Lord and among those who value that whole-scale concept of "peace."

The Tongue Lights a Raging Forest Fire

Besides those who actually die in a forest fire, the saddest thing that happens has to do with those who are forced out of their homes and have to flee for their lives. The good news comes with the perspective of time. Many of those people are able to rebuild their lives, often even their homes, and move ahead with even better lives, built upon their gratitude for their lives and what they learned in the painful process.

In Psalm 120, the writer, in the face of a raging firestorm of lies and deceit, finally emerges from the complacency and contentment of his state of spiritual denial. He now freely admits that he has been in that oblivious spiritual state far "too long" (Ps. 120:6). Having finally faced up to the reason for his escalating discontent, he is now willing to be displaced from his spiritual comfort zone and begin the pilgrim's journey. He now sees that his destination will be far better than anything he previously clung to and had to leave behind.

The Stopping of the Tongue

Though we might not readily admit it, many of us seem to believe that we have to stand up for ourselves in the face of unfair criticism. Perhaps some of us even think that secular assertiveness training can be "baptized" into a Christian concept. Jesus, however, certainly never defended Himself in such terms and, in fact, commanded us to "turn the other cheek." We are to take the "big picture" perspective on such abuse: "Vengeance is mine; I will repay, saith the Lord."

But, does the Lord, in real life, take care of the liar or slanderer and the treacherous deceiver? Obviously, there is no way of knowing the infinite variety of specific ways, and the precise timing, by which God dispenses His justice. However, for the Lord, who "shut the mouth of lions" (Heb. 11:33), it is no problem to silence an arrogant world ruler (Dan. 4:30-37) or to cause a couple of deceivers to drop dead (Acts 5:1-11) because they wouldn't own up to the truth.

At this point in our study of the pilgrim psalms, however, the key issue is not just that we can trust the Lord to defend us in the face of such unfair and ungodly lies and deceit. Rather, it is that we must not allow ourselves to get bogged down in the painful conflict and turned aside from the crucial journey that lies before us. Jesus warned that falling prey to "the worry of the world, and the deceitfulness of riches" causes spiritual unfruitfulness (Matt. 13:22). We must not, therefore, remain at the level of the world, or clinging to its ways, even if we have been guilty of temporarily sinking to that low estate.

The Dead Sea is the lowest place on the face of the earth, even lower than Death Valley in the desert of California. Most conservative biblical scholars believe that the "cities of the valley" (Gen. 13:12), including Sodom and Gomorrah, to which Lot and his family gravitated because of their attractiveness, are now buried beneath the deep and murky waters of the Dead Sea. It was only by leaving and beginning the rigors of the journey of ascent out of those depths that there was a future for Lot and what was left of his family. In fact, refusing to face and pursue the necessary journey proved fatal for Lot's wife (Gen. 19:26).

As noted earlier, all Jews, wherever they lived, were expected to go up to Jerusalem for the major feasts of the Jewish calendar. Since Jerusalem, and the Temple, after it was completed, were set on a hill and had to be approached on an upward grade, whether the pilgrimage brought them from the north, south, east or west, this is the nature of the spiritual growth charted in the Songs of Ascent. The question was not: "Do you have an uphill climb in front of you as you approach Jerusalem and the presence of the Lord?" Rather, for each individual, the reality was: "How long and how steep is the journey you must undertake to be rewarded by the blessing of the Lord's presence?"

That is the same question that we must ask as we seek to undertake our spiritual pilgrimage. Without question, whatever investment we make will pay worthwhile spiritual dividends. Nevertheless, the Lord reminds us that we must not take on the challenge of being His disciple, and growing in that relationship, as envisioned in the pilgrim psalms, without first "counting the cost" to see whether we are willing to commit the resources to see it through to the end (Luke 14:28).

A Journey of a Thousand Miles Begins

I have never run a marathon race. The reason I don't think I could run a marathon is that I couldn't motivate myself to leave the comfort of the starting line to undertake a race that long and exhausting. There wouldn't be enough at the finish to motivate me to begin, much less sustain me as the route, with its twists and turns, hills and valleys, stretched out in front of my tired legs.

Make no mistake: the pilgrim's journey of ascent is much closer to a spiritual "marathon" than a sprint. Yet, the discontent of life in a world that hates the peace that God offers is a great motivator. In addition, every step along the way offers refreshing fulfillment and gathering excitement and anticipation at what is around the next turn in the pilgrim's path that far outstrips the effort of the ascending climb.

As the ancient proverb says, "A journey of a thousand miles begins with the first step." Yes, it is true that pedaling the first leg did not guarantee that Lance Armstrong would negotiate the mountains and the weather and win the Tour de France. But, it is equally true that he could not win if he did not choose to leave the starting line and whole-heartedly face the looming challenges between him and circling the Champs-Elysees.

In conclusion, though it may be thought that a marathon run and the Tour de France are illustrations which overstate the stretching of the pilgrim's journey, it is worth pointing out one final thing about Psalm 120. The psalmist spoke of sojourning in "Meshech" and dwelling in "Kedar." As Boice correctly pinpoints things geographically, "Meshech" was located in what is today the area between northern Turkey, Kazakstan and Ukraine, while "Kedar" spoke of a Bedouin tribe in the Arabian Desert.[5] Thus, also Boice notes, it is impossible that the psalmist, even as a Diaspora Jew, could have lived in both places simultaneously and extremely unlikely that one person would have lived in both locales in the span of a lifetime, even as a trader.[6]

Nevertheless, the figurative usage of "Meshech" and "Kedar" by the psalmist does not detract from the sense of "distance" he is seeking to make. It would be like saying that "I've been so far away from the Lord that I feel like I'm in Timbuktu or Siberia." But, no matter how far it is, what is necessary is to say that I am now ready to make this journey. I'm the Lord's pilgrim. It is time to acknowledge complete dependence upon him.

Notes

[1] In this process of rethinking, the present writers have been actively involved, seeking not only a proper understanding of the structural angles involved, which helps greatly in focusing the emphasis of the passage in question, but also the practical/applicational implications of the structure for evangelical readers. Some of the more important works in which we have sought to clarify structural and/or applicational emphasis through the careful analysis of parallelism are A. Boyd Luter and Michelle V. Lee, "Philippians as Chiasmus," *New Testament Studies*, 1995; A. Boyd Luter and Kathy McReynolds, *Disciplined Living: What the New Testament Teaches about Discipleship and Recovery* (Grand Rapids: Baker, 1996); A. Boyd Luter and Barry C. Davis, *Ruth, Esther; Focus on the Bible* (Fearn, UK: Christian Focus, 2003); and Boyd Luter and Kathy McReynolds, *Women as Christ's Disciples Second Ed.* (Fearn, UK: Christian Focus, 2003).

[2] Willem Van Gemeren, "Psalms," in the *Expositor's Bible Commentary*, Vol. 5; Gen. Ed. Frank E. Gaebelein (Grand Rapids: Zondervan, 1991) p. 769.

[3] Francis Brown, S. R. Driver and C. A. Briggs, *A Hebrew and*

English Lexicon of the Old Testament (Oxford: Oxford University Press, 1972 corrected ed.) p. 1022.

[4] ibid., p. 771.

[5] James M. Boice, *Psalms: An Expositional Commentary*, Vol. 3 (Grand Rapids: Baker, 1998) p. 1073.

[6] ibid.

THREE

~~~~~~~~~~~~~~~~~~~~~~~~~~~~~~~~~~~~~~

"I Lift Up My Eyes to the Hills"
Dependence: Psalm 121-125

Godly Dependence: Strength for the
Journey

We discovered in the previous
chapter that the journey into
the Lord's presence begins
with feelings of discontentment. We
learned that discontentment in this context
is not necessarily a bad thing. In fact, it
makes perfect sense because when the
Lord's pilgrims dwell outside the Promised
Land, they, to a large degree, dwell in the
midst of those who are hostile to God. It

may initially be easy to feel content and secure in such an environment; but discontentment will inevitably set in. It will almost always be the case that, if we are sensitive to the Lord's leading, this discontentment can become a motivator to change. And so our conclusion is that the journey begins with discontentment.

The necessary next step in this upward progression is dependence. We are speaking of a specific kind of dependence, one that acknowledges our need for the *Lord's* provision and protection. Psalms 121-125 brilliantly reveal to us what it means to depend specifically on the Lord's provision and protection. We must first acknowledge our needs with joy and reverence for the Lord if we are to continue to progress (Pss. 121 and 122). The reason why this is so is that this kind of acknowledgment puts us in a place to receive God's mercy (Ps. 123). It opens our eyes to see His provision and it involves the deepest level of trust, which is the solid foundation of any relationship (Pss. 124 and 125).

We make this qualification concerning a specific kind of dependence because here in the affluent West, we are generally uncomfortable with the idea of "dependence." For us, dependence can mean weakness. We would rather view our dependencies as choices freely made. The reason for this is that we perceive choices to flow from our strength as individuals while we perceive dependence to show a weakness in character. Dependence viewed in this way threatens our individuality. And we must never underestimate the value we place on our individuality!

However, if we are honest enough with ourselves to see some of our "choices" for what they truly are (dependence), we are also in a place where we can admit that we can become dependent on many things which have little to do with our call to the sacred journey. It is far too easy in our technologically advanced culture to become dependent on entertainment, prescription drugs, and cosmetic surgeries to soothe our anxieties. Such dependence can truly be viewed as flowing from some kind of deficiency in character. The truth that Psalms 121-125 reveals to us is that godly dependence is a sign of true strength and individuality.

Dietrich Bonhoeffer captures this idea beautifully in his profound little book entitled *The Cost of Discipleship*. In it he makes a distinction between cheap grace and costly grace. Cheap grace *justifies sin* and encourages the sinner to stay as he or she is. Cheap grace allows one to follow a natural course and natural desires. Cheap grace correlates to dependency on the things of this world. In such a state one actually loses oneself and forfeits individuality. He or she just "goes with the flow".

Contrary to cheap grace, costly grace *justifies the sinner*. The justified sinner enters the world emptied of self. He or she follows Christ, pursuing holiness with reckless abandonment; he or she takes a stand against evil and resists his or her own will. With single-minded obedience, this justified sinner finds his or her self and gains individuality. This sounds difficult, I know. But the key is found in godly dependence.

Beyond the Hills: Psalm 121

As I said before, godly dependence involves first and foremost an acknowledgment of our genuine needs. Psalm 121 shows that our every need is met in the One who dwells beyond the hills. The historical context of this psalm reveals why it is so vital to look for help beyond what our physical eyes can see. The road leading up to Jerusalem was riddled with many dangers. The faithful pilgrims were subjected to extended exposure to the elements, which could cause severe illness; the threat of bandits dogged every step; the road itself, which often had loose stones and rubble, was nothing less than perilous.

When trouble came, where were the travelers to look but up to the hills which lay in front of them? And what did they see? They saw a beautiful and formidable natural fortress, a fortress which protected Jerusalem, one which King David had taken from the Jebusites (2 Sam. 5:7). It would have been tempting to trust in such a sight, especially in light of all the victories that had been won there in the name of the Lord. Eugene Peterson points out that the Hebrew would have also seen on those hills dozens of pagan shrines whose priests and priestesses would have offered all kinds of potions to protect from natural dangers.[1] This presented yet another reason for the traveler to trust in what he could clearly see.

Despite all of this there is a sense of anxiety in the psalmist's words, "where does my help come from?" (vv. 1b). The psalmist seems to sense that those hills, though they are majestic and awesome, are not what they appear to be: a refuge for the faithful. Instead they are a hiding place for all kinds of evildoers: robbers and vagabonds and worshipers of false gods, those who do great harm to devout travelers. It would be easy to be deceived by the beauty of the hills. But, reliance on the hills – on what the eyes see – will ultimately lead to disappointment.

Help, therefore, must come from beyond those hills, "My help comes from the Lord, the maker of heaven and earth" (vv. 2). The Lord is the Creator of the material world and, consequently, of the traveler, too. The Lord is therefore the Sustainer and Guardian of the traveler, "He will not let your foot slip—he who watches over you will not slumber; indeed, he who watches over Israel will neither slumber nor sleep. The Lord watches over you— the Lord is your shade at your right hand; the sun will not harm you by day nor the moon by night" (vv. 3-6).

Real needs must be met by real substance. Psalm 121 is not about the hills which offer counterfeit help to sustain the weary; it is about the Maker of the hills. The hills are mentioned only one time in this psalm while the Lord is referred to five times. Six times is He is called the Keeper of the faithful. If we are to be strong, we must depend on the One who sustains us and accompanies us on the journey. But this requires us to go beyond what we can see.

Reverent Dependence: Psalm 122

Nicholas Berdyaev was keenly aware of our modernist tendency to be shortsighted. He said that there is something morally repulsive about the modern activistic theories which deny contemplation and recognize nothing but struggle. For them not a single moment has value in itself, but is only a means for what follows. I think the point here is that our journey is more than just a struggle. If this is all we see, we have surely lost our way. Psalm 122 helps us to see beyond our present trials and setbacks and puts our progress in proper context. The focus in this psalm is on Zion, the city of Jerusalem, the goal of the pilgrimage. Zion is the center of God's judgment and peace and the worshipers are encouraged to continually pray for the peace of Zion. This psalm expresses the joy in Zion, with what has been referred to as "a pilgrim's warmth of religious emotion."

The pilgrim's joy is expressed in verses 1-2: "I rejoiced with those who said to me, 'Let us go to the house of the Lord.' Our feet are standing in your gates, O Jerusalem." The psalmist seems to be reflecting on the many times he has heard the call to go to the house of the Lord. At this point he is standing in Jerusalem and rejoicing that he has come so far. We are not even half way through the pilgrim psalms and the traveler is already at the gates of Zion. This is significant because it reveals that the richest part of the journey takes place *after* one has climbed the hill.

As we shall see, the road between the gate of Zion and the Temple is where the deepest part of spiritual growth takes place. This is why godly dependence is so necessary. And, as Psalm 122 reveals, dependence must be accompanied by joy, praise, and prayer. The joy expressed by the psalmist in verses 1-2 is a joy of anticipation. This is what he has been longing for. In verses 3-5, the pilgrim praises the Lord for the opportunity to go up to Jerusalem: "Jerusalem is built like a city that is closely compacted together. That is where the tribes go up, the tribes of the Lord, to praise the name of the Lord according to the statute given to Israel. There the thrones for judgment stand, the thrones of the house of David." In praise of Jerusalem, the psalmist sees all the worshipers of the Lord and the unity that is reflected in this gathering. This unity is accomplished not by the worshipers themselves, but by the One who called them together.

It is necessary for the pilgrims to be together at this point because the most fruitful part of the journey by far is about to take place. The feast cannot begin until the feet of the all pilgrims are standing in the gate. They must take this most important part of the journey together. The trip to the Temple can be an arduous one, requiring both unity and maturity. However, because of the burgeoning maturity of the pilgrim, the focus is not on the possible difficulties, but on the Lord. Praise is a sign of a maturing traveler who has arrived at Jerusalem. One of the overarching points of Psalm 122 is that praise, especially in the midst of difficulties, is an indication of spiritual growth!

In this context, prayer is also a sign of spiritual growth. Enemies lurk on the outside of Jerusalem and also within! When so many pilgrims gather together, prayer for peace is essential: "Pray for the peace of Jerusalem: 'May those who love you be secure. May there be peace within your walls and security within your citadels.' For the sake of my brothers and friends, I will say, 'Peace be within you.' For the sake of the house of the Lord our God, I will seek your prosperity" (vv. 6-9).

In his letter to the Ephesians, the letter best known for its emphasis on unity and its teachings on spiritual maturity, the Apostle Paul seems to stress this threefold division of joy, praise, and prayer. Throughout the letter Paul expresses joy and praise to God for all the spiritual blessings we have in Christ. He also prays consistently for the saints that they will be unified and that they will continue to mature in Christ. One of the central messages of Ephesians is that we need each other in order to reach the heights of maturity in Christ. Psalm 122 echoes this same truth. Nothing short of complete dependence on the Lord and his saints can make the journey possible at this point.

Where are You Looking? Psalm 123

It is at this stage that dependence comes most clearly into focus. In Psalm 121, the pilgrim "looks to the hills." In Psalm 123, as the faithful traveler stands at the gate of Zion, the hills are behind him. He sees the Temple, but his attention is drawn toward heaven, "I lift up my eyes to you, to you whose throne is in heaven. As the eyes of slaves look to the hand of their master, as the eyes of a maid look to the hand of her mistress, so our eyes look to the Lord our God, till he shows us his mercy" (vv. 1-2).

Where we *look* reveals a lot about who we are and what we desire. I love to watch tennis. In the summertime I wait anxiously for each event. I read all the articles on the internet. I look at all the draws to see where my favorite player is seeded. I constantly think about who may win a certain tournament, given the kind of surface it is played upon. Everyone who knows me well knows exactly where they can find me when tennis season is in full swing. Either I am at a local tournament or I am watching one on television.

Now, my love for tennis not only shapes my character, but to some degree, it also flows from my character. I like tennis because I like competition and discipline. I am competitive and disciplined; therefore I like sports. Tennis just happens to be one of my favorite sports. I also like to read. What I choose to read flows from my character and, in turn, shapes my character. Thank the Lord that I have matured enough to choose books which help me to think deeply about my faith.

The point of what I am trying to say is that what or who we look at or look to can reveal much about our heart. In the opening verses of Psalm 123, the writer mentions "eyes" four times. His eyes look to Him who dwells in heaven. As the eyes of slaves and of maids look to their masters and mistresses, so the eyes of the pilgrims who stand in the gate of Zion look to the Lord their God. Their priorities are right. They know where goodness is found.

What is more, this dependence on the Lord puts them in the proper place to receive his mercy: "Have mercy on us, O Lord, have mercy on us, for we have endured much contempt. We have endured much ridicule from the proud, much contempt from the arrogant" (vv. 3-4). What is interesting about this passage is that the psalmist is possibly standing in the gates of Jerusalem and is still concerned about the taunts of his enemies. What is probably more disturbing is the idea that the gates of Jerusalem do not necessarily shield us from words of the proud and arrogant. In fact, we may feel their taunts in a deeper way because we are nearer to the Holy One. In this case, the need for divine help arises out of a deep awareness of the evil that can harass those who are on the sacred journey.

The proud and arrogant do not look to God to meet their needs. They depend only upon themselves. The one dependent on the Lord does not look to these troublemakers for favor and relief. They are "slaves" of the Lord and look to Him alone to deliver them and to protect them from further harm. The Lord, in turn, "sees" and protects His faithful.

The Lord Sees: Protection and Provision: Ps. 124

In his monumental work, *The Institutes of the Christian Religion*, John Calvin keenly observes the nature of God's protection and provision. He implores us to remember that providence means much more than the idea that God is up in heaven watching what is taking place on earth – that he just simply oversees all world events. When God told Abraham that he would provide for him, he meant not merely that he foreknew Abraham's future and would meet him there, but that he would manage all things for him and bring all things to a good end.

The Lord is active in the lives of those who journey toward Him. In Psalm 124, the pilgrims reflect on the many perils and trials from which God has delivered them and this reflection moves them to give thanks:

> If the Lord had not been on our side—
> let Israel say—
> If the Lord had not been on our side
> when men attacked us,
> when their anger flared against us,
> they would have swallowed us alive;
> the flood would have engulfed us,
> the torrent would have swept over us,
> the raging waters would have swept us away.
> Praise be to the Lord,
> who has not let us be torn by their teeth.
> We have escaped like a bird
> out of the fowler's snare;
> the snare has been broken,
> and we have escaped.
> Our help is in the name of the Lord,
> the Maker of heaven and earth.

The themes of providence and protection are prominent in this psalm. They are revealed most clearly in this inverted structure:

> The providence of the Lord (vv. 1-2a)
> Protection from Dangers (vv. 2b-5)
> *Praise to the Lord (v. 6a)*
> *Protection from Dangers (vv. 6b-7)*
> *The providence of the Lord (v. 8)*

The themes of God's providence and protection begin and conclude this incredible psalm. What is most amazing is that the closer we draw to the Temple, the more prominent these themes become. When we "dwell in Meshech," it may be easier to believe that we can actually care for and protect ourselves. We are far from the majesty of Him who holds our lives in His hands. When we are close to his Temple we realize in a deeper way his providence and protection precisely because we finally understand the nature of the evil which confronts us. Psalm 124 shows forth the many unpleasant aspects of life. We are constantly threatened by all kinds of uncertainties – and these uncertainties are real and possible. The most natural thing for us to do today is to look to medicine or psychology for help. Psalm 124 is an example of one who fearlessly faces evil, and finds God there as an ever present help. Trouble opens our spiritual eyes to see God's hand in protection and provision. When this reality finally hits home with us, the result is inner strength and peace.

Strength and Godly Dependence: Psalm 125

We began this chapter by discussing the strength required to depend on the Lord. We end it by looking at the true source of inner strength: unshakable confidence in the Lord by whose judgment the powers of the unrighteous is removed. This unshakable confidence brings peace:

> Those who trust in the Lord are like Mount Zion,
> which can never be shaken but endures forever.
> As the mountains surround Jerusalem,

so the Lord surrounds his people
both now and forevermore.
The scepter of the wicked will not remain
over the land allotted to the righteous,
for then the righteous might use
their hands to do evil.
Do good, O Lord, to those who are good,
to those who are upright in heart.
But those who turn to crooked ways
the Lord will banish with the evildoers.
Peace be upon Israel.

The inverted structure of this psalm reveals more clearly this process:

Inner Strength (v. 1)
   Confidence in the Lord's Help (v. 2)
      Confidence in the Triumph over Evil (v. 3)
   Prayer for the Lord's Help (vv. 4-5b)
Peace (v. 5)

On top of the hills, the pilgrim gains a perspective on life that allows inner strength to flow. Mount Zion was not the highest peak around Jerusalem. However, surrounded by the mountains, Zion rested secure. The psalmist compares the Lord to the hills surrounding Jerusalem and the people to Mount Zion. The Lord is around his people *"both now and forevermore."* This truth can only be embraced by those who have climbed the hills.

This reality brings us full circle to the blessing bestowed on the pilgrims in Psalm 121:

> The Lord will keep you from all harm—
> he will watch over your life;
> the Lord will watch over your coming and going
> *both now and forevermore.*

What a promise! This promise is only surpassed by the reality that heavenly blessings will far transcend these given for those who dwell on earth. Dependence on the Lord's provision and protection is necessary for a successful journey into the presence of the Lord. Dependence involves first a genuine acknowledgment of our legitimate needs. It must be accompanied by reverence because this puts us in a place of humility; and humility leads to mercy. Most importantly, dependence opens our spiritual eyes to see God's hand in our daily affairs. This is nothing short of true illumination.

Notes

[1] Eugene Peterson, *A Long Obedience in the Same Direction: Discipleship in an Instant Society*, (Downers Grove: IVP, 1980), p. 36.

FOUR

~~~~~~~~~~~~~~~~~~~~~~~~~~~~~~~~~~~~~~

"The Lord has Done Great Things for Us"
Illumination: Psalms 126-129

Do Not Forget!

There is something about prosperity that causes one to lose perspective. When things are going well, we tend to want to take credit for it. When our career is going well and money is no problem, we attribute it to hard work. When we win an athletic event, we take the credit for having been disciplined. When we get good grades in school, we are proud of ourselves for having put out the effort. When our children are well-behaved, we figure that we must have done something right.

Well, there is no question that we do play a role in our successes. However, this is only half the truth. The entire truth is that the Lord has everything to do with our success. This is the lesson of Deuteronomy 8. If we say to ourselves, "My power and the strength of my hands have produced this wealth for me," (Deut. 8:17) we are not living in accordance with reality. We have forgotten who we are. But, most importantly, we have forgotten who He is. "But remember the Lord your God, for it is he who gives the ability to produce wealth, and so confirms his covenant" (Deut. 8:18a).

In the desert east of the Jordan, the Israelites stood poised to enter the Promised Land. Their forefathers, who had wandered forty years in the desert because of their disobedience, had all died off. So Moses, in the Book of Deuteronomy, is repeating the commands and requirements of the Lord to this generation. Moses sternly warns the Israelites not to forget the Lord after they enter the land.

He tells them to "Observe the commands of the Lord your God, walking in his ways and revering him. For the Lord your God is bringing you into a good land — a land with streams and pools of water, with springs flowing in the valleys and hills; a land with wheat and barley, vines and fig trees, pomegranates, olive oil and honey; a land where bread will not be scarce and you will lack nothing; a land where the rocks are iron and you can dig copper out of the hills. When you have eaten and are satisfied, praise the Lord your God for the good land he has given you. Be careful that you do not forget the Lord your God, failing to observe his commands, his laws and his decrees that I am giving you this day. Otherwise, when you eat and are satisfied, when you build fine houses and settle down, and when your herds and flocks grow large and your silver and gold increase and all you have is multiplied, then your heart will become proud and you will forget the Lord your God, who brought you out of Egypt, out of the land of slavery. He led you through the vast and dreadful desert, that thirsty and waterless land, with its venomous snakes and scorpions. He brought you water out of hard rock. He gave you manna to eat in the desert, something your fathers had never known, to humble and to test you so that in the end it might go well with you. You may say to yourself,

> My power and the strength of my hands have produced this wealth for me." *But remember the Lord you God, for it is he who gives you the ability to produce wealth, and so confirms his covenant, which he swore to your forefathers, as it is today.*

The message of Deuteronomy 8:6-18 is rather simple: *the things that truly bring wealth and happiness come not from hard work and discipline alone, but from the Lord God, who gives his people the ability to accomplish these things according to his covenant promises. Therefore, do not forget him.* Every earthly blessing the Israelites could have ever wanted was built into the covenant. In fact, later on in Deuteronomy a more precise list of those blessings appears. If the Israelites obeyed the voice of the Lord, they would simply be blessed in every facet of life. The Lord would withhold no favor — his people would experience the bounties of his mercy and love.

The Israelites' role was to obey the requirements of the covenant and to acknowledge the One from whom all blessings flow. However, as Joshua, Judges, 1 and 2 Samuel, and 1 and 2 Kings reveal, the Israelites failed to keep their end of the covenant. They were lured by the surrounding nations to believe that happiness and wealth are of human origin alone. Their shortsightedness cost them the promised land. Their history is riddled with destruction and banishment.

Psalms 126-129 deal with a crucial part of the pilgrim's journey: illumination. Illumination dispels all illusion. It is at this stage that the pilgrim realizes in the depths of his or her soul that "the Lord has done great things for them" (Ps. 126:2b). They come to grips with the fact that, though they may have been woefully unfaithful to God, He has remained true. Hence, illumination is the natural next step in the journey. Godly dependence precedes illumination because it is dependence which opens our hearts and brings us to a place where we can embrace God's mercy. The "illumination" of his mercy enables us to see life for what it really is — in all its hardships and in all its blessings. We understand life more clearly at this point because we have grown closer to the One who oversees all. We have cleared the hills and moved closer to His Temple. This is the process which unfolds in Psalms 126-129.

"Captives" and Reality: Psalm 126

Psalm 126 begins with the statement, "When the Lord brought back the captives to Zion, we were like men who dreamed. Our mouths were filled with laughter, our tongues with songs of joy" (vv. 1-2a). The interesting word here is *captive*. Israel spent much of its time as a nation serving other gods and they became as wicked as those whom they had served. This is why the Lord finally banished them from the land of Canaan (the northern kingdom in 722 BC and the southern kingdom in 586 BC).

When the Israelites were carried to foreign lands to serve those foreign gods, they quickly realized that life with them was not what they expected it to be. They were expecting wealth and happiness. And they were duped into believing that wealth and happiness could be found solely on their own. But in retrospect, as they stood near the Temple, they acknowledged that the Lord brought back *captives* to Zion. Captives are prisoners. They are neither happy nor wealthy! The great lesson here is that when the faithful wander from Zion, they become enslaved. Freedom, and the wealth and happiness it can bring, can only be found at the Temple in Zion. This is why their "mouths were filled with laughter and their tongues with songs of joy" (v. 2). They were finally free.

It is significant that joy is mentioned four times in this psalm:

> When the Lord brought back the captives to Zion,
> we were like men who dreamed.

61

Our mouths were filled with laughter,
our tongues with *songs of joy*.
Then it was said among the nations,
"The Lord has done great things for them."
The Lord has done great things for us,
and we are *filled with joy*.
Restore our fortunes, O Lord,
like streams in the Negev.
Those who sow in tears
will reap with *songs of joy*.
He who goes out weeping,
carrying seed to sow,
will return with *songs of joy*,
carrying sheaves with him.

It is also striking that, in verses 5 and 6, songs of joy are juxtaposed with *tears* and *weeping*. The work may be laborious and the results uncertain, but the important point is that the Lord will be with his people and will ultimately bless them.[1] He is faithful to his covenant. It is against his nature to be otherwise. The blessings in verses 5 and 6 are actually an answer to the prayer in verse 4. This prayer is possibly a reflection on the harshness of the Israelites' existence in the foreign land. So they pray for a continuation of "restoration" and God answers them in accordance with his promise to be faithful.

John Calvin sees in this psalm a timeless truth. He points out that we must learn to apply our minds to the incredible truth that exudes from this psalm; that is, God will not only wipe away every tear, but will also fill our hearts with joy inconceivable.

Thus, as they stand on Mount Zion, the pilgrims realize they are captives no more. They have returned home. They cannot be anything but joyful. The world had captivated them, but now they have come to their senses. Now, this may not make sense to the world, but, even in the midst of hardship, the faithful rest in the truth that the Lord has done great things for them. It is only when we embrace this truth that joy can overtake us.

The House that God Builds: Psalms 127 and 128

The illumination process continues as the pilgrims stand before the House of God. It is easy to imagine how the sight of the Temple could cause one to reflect on one's own house: Does God dwell in *my* house? What does He have to do with *my* family? What I think is being implicitly communicated here is that there is something about ascending into the presence of the Lord that causes us to journey inward, that causes us to evaluate our own lives more realistically. We become more willing to ask the hard questions, and, most importantly, to hear and to heed the answers.

The answer that Psalms 127 and 128 provide is this: *If the faithful would desire to be more God-centered in their everyday lives, they must resist the temptation to build a "house" (raise a family and all that this entails: provision, protection, etc.), unless they first trust unswervingly in the Lord.* Now, intuitively, we know this and believe it to be true. However, we cannot fully grasp the magnitude of this truth until we understand the overall content and structure of these two psalms:

Psalm 127

Unless the Lord builds the house,
its builders labor in vain.
Unless the Lord watches over the city,
the watchmen stand guard in vain.
In vain you rise early
and stay up late,
toiling for food to eat—
for he grants sleep to those he loves.
Sons are a heritage from the Lord,
children a reward from him.
Like arrows in the hands of a warrior
are sons born in one's youth.
Blessed is the man
whose quiver is full of them.
They will not be put to shame
when they contend with their enemies in the gate.

Psalm 128

Blessed are all who fear the Lord,
who walk in his ways.
You will eat the fruit of your labor;
blessings and prosperity will be yours.
Your wife will be like a fruitful vine
within your house;
your sons will be like olive shoots
around your table.
Thus is the man blessed who fears the Lord.

Futility and Blessing (Ps. 127:1-2)
God's Blessing on the Family (Ps. 127:3-5

The Blessing of a God-Fearing Family (Ps. 128:1-4)
Prosperity and Blessing (Ps. 128:5-6)

Several things stand out in light of the content and structure of these psalms. First, these psalms belong to the wisdom genre and are meant to evoke a response of wisdom in the wise.[2] Second, the psalmist extends God's sovereignty over man's futile existence (Ps. 127:1-2). It's not that he belittles hard work and toil; but, to live simply to provide for self and family is a fruitless way to live. The wise are encouraged to live in a higher way by trusting the Lord first and foremost in their work. The blessing of God is on the labor of the godly; thus there is no anguish (Ps. 127:2; Ps. 128:1-2). "Anguish is that experience by which work is turned into toil. Human labor under the sun becomes toil when God's blessing is absent."[3]

Third, blessing on blessing is heaped upon the God-fearing family. Not only are children themselves an inheritance from the Lord (Ps. 127:3), but they also seem to provide a level of protection and security to the godly family (127:4-5)! The wife is blessed and the children prosper (Ps. 128:3). These blessings on the family extend to "all the days of your life" (Ps. 128:5). These blessings do not stop at the family, but apply to Jerusalem and all of Israel (Ps. 128:5-6). If you'll remember, this same idea is communicated in slightly different language in Psalm 125:2, "As the mountains surround Jerusalem, so the Lord surrounds his people both now and forevermore."

In contrast to life under God's blessing, Jacque Ellul once commented on fruitless labor "under the sun alone." He said that the first great fact which emerges from our civilization is that today everything has become "means." There is no longer an "end"; we do not know whither we are going. We have forgotten our collective end, and we possess great means: we set huge machines in motion in order to arrive nowhere.

For those who are not willing to make the sacred pilgrimage, life is essentially characterized by means without an end. For the wise and the faithful, though, labor is not vain. We have an end, and that end is the Lord, who builds our house and blesses it abundantly. Indeed, the Lord has done great things for us!

While the blessing of the Lord is on the righteous, it is far from the unrighteous, from those who hate Zion. But the enemies of Zion do play a role in the pilgrim's journey.

Remember! Psalm 129

We began this chapter with the encouragement from Deuteronomy 8 to never forget the Lord. We end it with an exhortation from Psalm 129 to remember our enemies:

> They have greatly oppressed me from my youth—
> let Israel say—
> they have greatly oppressed me from my youth,
> but they have not gained the victory over me.
> Plowmen have plowed my back

and made their furrows long.
But the Lord is righteous;
he has cut me free from the cords of the wicked.
May all who hate Zion
be turned back in shame.
May they be like grass on the roof,
which withers before it can grow;
with it the reaper cannot fill his hands,
nor the one who gathers fill his arms.
May those who pass by not say,
"The blessing of the Lord by upon you;
we bless you in the name of the Lord."

The confidence which the Israelites have in the Lord is based on his past deliverances. The mention of enemies in this psalm is based on a deep concern for God's kingdom. Those who "hate Zion" are those who care nothing for God or his promises. According to Van Gemeren, "Zion denotes here the Lord's presence among his people, his covenant and blessing, and the hope in the victorious establishment of God's kingdom."[4] The major theme of Psalm 126, the Lord has done great things for us, testifies that the Lord is a God who keeps his covenant. And all of the blessings of the covenant are bestowed on the godly.

Those who hate Zion are against God. What is important to note here is that this curse on the wicked has nothing to do with personal revenge. It has to do with asking for God's vindication of the righteous. It is a righteous indignation. For those who are ascending into the Lord's presence, God's kingdom and glory are their main concern. Jesus, in His Sermon on the Mount, also echoes this truth, "But seek first his kingdom and his righteousness, and all these things will be given to you as well" (Matt. 6:33).

However, there is a tension when we think about the content of Psalm 129 and Jesus' teachings on the ways in which we should treat our enemies. In the same Sermon on the Mount, Jesus said, "You have heard that is was said, 'Love your neighbor and hate your enemy.' But I tell you: Love your enemies and pray for those who persecute you, that you may be sons of your Father in heaven" (5:44-45a). The Apostle Paul also commanded that we bless and not curse our enemies (Rom. 12:14, 17-21).

A couple of things can be said in this context. First, it is important to keep in mind that the focus of Psalm 129 is on the God who delivers and who vindicates the righteous. As we said earlier, the godly are deeply concerned for God's kingdom and glory. So they cry out to God to deliver them, to vindicate them, and to establish his kingdom. Those who have ascended the holy mount can do nothing else but be consumed with concern for these things.

Second, mature New Testament believers are actually empowered by the Spirit to move beyond mere "concern for God's kingdom" to love. This certainly does not mean that we contradict the content of Psalm 129.[5] But we move beyond the desire for the honor of God's kingdom in the face of his enemies to genuine sacrificial love for the enemies themselves. Therefore, we pray for our enemies with two things in mind: 1) we remember that we ourselves were once enemies of God and were shown mercy (Rom. 5:8); 2) God desires all persons to come to a saving knowledge of Christ (1 Tim. 2:3-6).

Thus, we remember our enemies for three reasons: 1) we were once like them; 2) God deeply desires them to join us in the sacred pilgrimage into His presence; 3) Because we were once like them, our enemies constantly remind us that the "Lord has done great things for us!" This is by far one of the most important points to be made in this psalm. We *must* remember that we were once as our enemies are. It is almost like a command. For this realization, and this one alone, brings about in us a deep sense of the need for confession and humility.

Notes

[1]Willem A. Van Gemeren, *The Expositor's Bible Commentary*, Volume 5, *Psalms*, Frank Gaebelein, ed. (Grand Rapids: Zondervan, 1991), p. 792.

[2]ibid., p. 793.

[3]ibid., p. 794.

[4]Van Germeren, p. 799.

[5]Much more could be said about the "curse" passages in these and other psalms. But this goes beyond the scope of this book. For a deeper analysis of this issue, we encourage you to consult any of the solid evangelical commentaries on the Psalms.

FIVE

~~~~~~~~~~~~~~~~~~~~~~~~~~~~~~~~~~~~~~~

"Out of the Depths ..."
Confession and Humility: Psalms 130-131

The Only Proper Response

St Augustine of Hippo (354-430) was one of the most profound and influential theologians in the history of the church. He wrote extensively on many subjects, including theology, philosophy and biblical doctrines. One of Augustine's most inspiring works is his *Confessions*. In it he describes in detail his conversion experience. The following is a rather lengthy, but worthy, excerpt which enables us to peer very briefly inside this pilgrim's heart:

Why then should I be concerned for human readers to hear my confessions? It is not they who are going to "heal my sicknesses" (Ps. 102:3). The human race is inquisitive about other people's lives, but negligent to correct their own. Why do they demand to hear from me what I am when they refuse to hear from you what they are? And when they hear me talking about myself, how can they know if I am telling the truth, when no one "knows what is going on in a person except the human spirit which is within (I Cor. 2:11)? ...

Nevertheless, make it clear to me, physician of my most intimate self, that good results from my present undertaking. Stir up the heart when people read and hear the confessions of my past wickedness, which you have forgiven and covered up to grant me happiness in yourself, transforming my soul by faith and your sacrament. ...

My Lord, every day my conscience makes confession, relying on the hope of your mercy as more to be trusted than its own innocence. So what profit is there, I ask when, to human readers, by this book I confess to you who I now am, not what I once was? The profit derived from confessing my past I have seen and spoken about. But what I now am at this time when I am writing my confessions many wish to know, both those who know me and those who do not but have heard something from me or about me. ...

But what edification do they hope to gain by this? Do they desire to join me in thanksgiving when they hear how, by your gift, I have come close to you, and do they pray for me when they hear how I am held back by my own weight? To such sympathetic readers I will indeed reveal myself. ...

When I am confessing not what I was but what I am now, the benefit lies in this: I am making this confession not only before you with a secret exaltation and fear and with a secret grief touched by hope, but also in the ears of believing sons of men, sharers in my joy, conjoined with me in mortality, my fellow citizens and pilgrims, some who have gone before, some who follow after, and some who are my companions in this life. ...

Accordingly, let me confess what I know of myself. Let me confess too what I do not know of myself. For what I know of myself I know because you grant me light, and what I do not know of myself, I do not know until such time as my darkness becomes "like noonday" before your face (Isa. 58:10). ...[1]

In speaking of his own conversion experience, the Apostle Paul says this, "Here is a trustworthy saying that deserves full acceptance: Christ Jesus came into the world to save sinners—of whom I am the worst. But for that very reason I was shown mercy so that in me, the worst of sinners, Christ Jesus might display his unlimited patience as an example for those who would believe on him and receive eternal life" (1 Tim. 1:15-16). Augustine is following in the footsteps of Paul and demonstrating through his own testimony that God does indeed save the worst of sinners.

What Paul and Augustine teach us is that the proper response to the amazing reality of God's salvation is confession and humility. The point is that their confession and humility express the profound truths found in Psalm 130 and 131. Martin Luther called these psalms, together with other penitential psalms, "Pauline Psalms" because of their focus on the gravity of sin, the weight of guilt, and confidence in God.

Confession and Humility: Psalms 130 and 131

The central message of Psalms 130 and 131 is that the God who dwells in Zion not only provides spiritual and physical blessings (previous chapter), but he also forgives sin:

Psalm 130
Out of the depths I cry to you, O Lord;
O Lord, hear my voice.
Let your ears be attentive
to my cry for mercy.
If you, O Lord, kept a record of sins,
O Lord, who could stand?
But with you there is forgiveness;
therefore, you are feared.
I wait for the Lord, my soul waits,
and in his word I put my hope.
My soul waits for the Lord
more than watchmen wait for the morning,
more than watchmen wait for the morning.
O Israel, put your hope in the Lord,
for with the Lord is unfailing love
and with him is full redemption.
He himself will redeem Israel from all their sins.

Psalm 131
My heart is not proud, O Lord,
my eyes are not haughty;
I do not concern myself with great matters

or things too wonderful for me.
But I have stilled and quieted my soul;
like a weaned child with its mother,
like a weaned child is my soul within me.
O Israel, put your hope in the Lord
both now and forevermore.

The main point of these two psalms can be visualized in an inverted structure:

Lament (vv. 1-2)
    Confession of Sin (vv. 3-4)
        Waiting for the Lord (vv. 5-6)
    Forgiveness of Sin (vv. 7-8)
Humility (Ps. 131:1-3)

The closer pilgrims come to the Temple, the more they become aware of their sin (Ps. 130:1-2). The Lord is the only one who can forgive sin; therefore, He is to be greatly feared (Ps. 130:3-4). Because He is the One who will forgive sin, He is not only to be feared, but He is to be waited upon (Ps. 130:5-6). The emphasis in this passage on "wait" and "watchmen" brings out the importance of this point. He will indeed forgive his faithful ones (Ps. 130:7-8). Hence, to such glorious realities, confession and humility are the only proper response (Ps. 131:1-3).

One of the most difficult things for a pilgrim to do is to wait, especially since he or she has traveled so far. But there is something about the wait that brings maturity. There are many passages in Scripture which discuss the benefit of waiting for the Lord[2]; but two are worth mentioning in this context. David, in Psalm 27, tells of the taunts of his enemies. While waiting for the Lord to deliver him, he says this, "I am still confident of this; I will see the goodness of the Lord in the land of the living. Wait for the Lord; be strong and take heart and wait for the Lord" (Ps. 27:13-14). We know that David, because he was trained and disciplined while waiting upon the Lord, became the greatest king Israel had ever known. Hebrews 11 is full of pilgrims who waited by faith for the promises of God to be fulfilled. They did not see them fulfilled in their lifetime; however, waiting upon the Lord, they never wavered in their faith. This was a sign of their maturity and also the process by which they matured.

The focus of these Psalms 130 and 131, then, is the pilgrim's journey out of darkness and into the light. Psalm 129 recalls the sorrows through which the travelers passed — the oppression they experienced from their enemies. Now they are distressed by their own sins. For what had they brought out of the darkness but their own sins and iniquities? There can be no hope of salvation until the traveler is brought to experience his or her own guilt. To be in this place, then, is a necessary and blessed experience when it is prompted by the work of the Holy Spirit. When in this darkness the pilgrims turn to the Lord, the light of day begins to dawn upon them.

The conviction of sin and turning to the Lord cannot be underestimated in this context. Therefore Psalm 130:3-4 deserves special attention. First there is a confession of the holiness of God (v. 3), and then what follows is a confession of the reverence which is due him based on his holiness. This is to put God and us in our proper place. What develops from this realization is an incredible confidence of faith. This is evident in the next two verses: "I wait for the Lord, my soul waits, and in his word I hope. My soul waits for the Lord more than the watchman waits for the morning" (vv. 5-6). Such waiting could only spring from a confidence of faith. The word translated "wait" actually means "to hope that a thing will be effected, and to wait steadily and patiently till it is effected." It is a waiting from which all doubt is dispelled and from which hope exudes.

The psalmist then urges the pilgrim to hope in the Lord, for with him is mercy and redemption (vv. 7-8). He encourages the pilgrim to not let present sorrows cause doubt for one moment. The psalmist sees through the eyes of faith the clearing sky and with it, the unchanging nature of God's mercy and grace. He has learned the vital lesson that God will act not according to our needs, but according to his nature. Therefore, our confidence and hope stand secure because mercy does not depend upon us, but upon him who never changes.

Psalm 131 is a continuation of this theme. The confidence of faith and hope leads to humility and a weaned spirit. Humility and meekness are the two moral traits which most characterized the Lord Jesus himself when he was on earth. He modeled them in order to present to us the pathway to finding rest for our souls. Nothing speaks so powerfully of the work of grace than humility. It is a sure sign of the sanctifying power of the truth and a true indication of spiritual maturity. The lower we go, the closer we grow in conformity to Him. This is indeed a hard lesson today considering the high value we place on independence. But it is a necessary lesson to learn.

The humble pilgrim does not concern himself or herself with great matters or things too high and lofty. He or she leaves all management of these things in the hands of the Lord. Thus, the humble pilgrim waits patiently for the Lord and is satisfied with his arrangements. Nothing goes against the modern mindset more than waiting! However, this is one of the primary reasons why the peace we so long for often eludes us. We have not fully grasped the spiritual truth that the peace that passes all understanding is only realized in the waiting. The pilgrim who has learned the art of humility in this way is characterized by two things: 1) he or she has learned to quiet his or her soul; 2) he or she is as a weaned child (v. 2). The stilled and quieted soul of the weaned does not come easily. It requires watchfulness and spiritual energy in order to maintain the weaned state. Just as a child is accustomed to looking to his or her mother for nourishment, so the pilgrim, if he or she is not vigilant, will be tempted to fall back into old ways of thinking and acting. He or she will be tempted, as it were, to retreat down the mountain.

Mature, that is humble and weaned pilgrims, are those who have found what God is for his people, what he is in his grace for them when they have passed through their sorrow for their sin. Thus redeemed from their transgressions and delivered from the power of their enemies, the Lord has become the strength of their hearts. They have been "weaned" from everything else. They have discovered a faith without trappings. It is a spiritual awakening far beyond anything this world could ever understand. And only those who are truly humble can desire it.

Having found for himself that the Lord can be trusted at all times, that none who wait for him will be denied, the psalmist exhorts the pilgrim to never give up confidence in the Lord. He is the one who will never disappoint. He may bring his people into trials, but he will never forsake them. Therefore, the psalmist says, "put your hope in the Lord both now and forevermore" (v. 3).

The Roman philosopher, Boethius, wrote a penetrating little book entitled, *The Consolation of Philosophy*. As the main character of the book, Boethius was suffering from an illness in which he had forgotten who he was. He was told by Lady Philosophy that if he wanted the doctor's help, he must reveal his wound. This is exactly what Boethius, following the lead of the psalmist, does. In every age, dependence, confession, and humility are the characteristics of a true pilgrim.

Anselm, the Archbishop of Canterbury from 1093 to 1109, was an author whose writings were highly influential in the development of theology in Western Christianity. In his sophisticated, yet profoundly devotional work, *Proslogion*, Anselm describes his own experience of confession of sin and waiting on the Lord:

> Alas, unfortunate that I am, one of the miserable children of Eve, separated from God. What have I undertaken? What have I actually done? Where was I going? Where

have I come to? To what was I aspiring? For what do I yearn? "I sought goodness" [Ps. 121:1] and, lo, "there is confusion" [Jer. 14:19]. I yearned for God, and I was in my own way. I sought peace within myself and "I have found tribulation and sadness" in my heart of hearts [Ps. 114:3]. I wished to laugh from out of the happiness of my soul, and "the sobbing of my heart" [Ps. 37:9] makes me cry out. I hoped for gladness and, lo, my sighs come thick and fast… Let me discern Your light whether it be from afar or from the depths. Teach me to seek You, and reveal Yourself to me as I seek, because I can neither seek You if You do not teach me how, nor find You unless You reveal Yourself. Let me seek You in desiring You; let me desire You in seeking You; let me find You in loving You; let me love You in finding You.[3]

We must always remember that depths have a bottom, but the heights are boundless. Therefore we must do what it takes to develop the art of waiting and hoping in the Lord. The Lord unabashedly assures his faithful pilgrims that confession and humility have eternal benefits: "In repentance and rest is your salvation, in quietness and trust is your strength" (Isa. 30:15a).

This waiting process is an integral part of the journey; for it gives us the opportunity to meditate on all His promises.

Notes
[1]Augustine, *Confessions*, trans. by Henry Chadwick, (Oxford, Oxford University Press, 1991), pp. 180-183, 202.

[2]For a few examples, see Pss. 25:5, 104:27-28, 145:15-16; Jer. 14:22; Luke 2:25; I Cor. 1:7; I Thess. 1:10, Jas. 5:7.

[3]Anselm, *Anselm Of Canterbury: The Major Works*, edited by Brain Davies and G.R. Evans, (Oxford: Oxford University Press, 1998), pp. 86-87.

SIX

~~~~~~

"O Lord, Remember David!"
Meditation on God's Promises: Psalm 132

Awkwardness

We have all at one time or another dealt with feelings of awkwardness. I am very petite, and when I was a child, I was always the last one picked when it came to team sports. I longed to fit in and to be like everyone else, but it just did not happen. I tried to prove my worth by doing things which would compensate for my size. But when it came right down to it, I was always overlooked. There is nothing worse when you are a child than feeling out of place. My experience did, however, make me much more sensitive to others who were left out. I went out of my way to make them feel wanted and cared for. I wanted them to know that they did have a purpose, even if others did not see it.

The Mystery of the Out-of-Place Psalm

Psalm 132 is the "awkward child" of the Psalms of Ascent. It is at least twice as long as any of the other pilgrim psalms. Although it is not the only one that mentions David (Psalm 122 does, but only once), Psalm 132 does so by name four times in the span of eighteen verses. In addition, Psalm 132 is alone among the grouping that reflects back on David's role in preparing for the building of the Temple and the covenant the Lord made with David and his descendants.

In the thinking of not a few reputable biblical experts, given its size and distinctive subject matter, it is something of a mystery why Psalm 132 is even included in the Psalms of Ascent. But is it necessary to have a big question mark hanging over the placement and role of Psalm 132 within the pilgrim psalms? Or are there other factors to be considered, some of which may even help us appreciate the historical and spiritual importance of this unique group of psalms even more?

Focusing on the Last Part of the Journey

Psalm 132 is the thirteenth of the fifteen Psalms of Ascent (i.e., Psalms 120-134). That would place its singing *relatively near* the end, but not *at* the end, of the journey that the pilgrims would be undertaking to Jerusalem for the great feasts. Thus, as they neared the city of Jerusalem, dusty and exhausted, as they looked up at David's capital city, they would be refreshed as they sang and remembered the promises the Lord had made to David and the events that led to the Temple being built.

In a very real sense, what was taking place with the pilgrims as they thought about, and mediated on, what they were singing as they neared Jerusalem at the season of the feast, was a re-enactment. Much as the ark had been taken up to Jerusalem over those roads in 2 Samuel 6, the pilgrims were not just remembering, but virtually reliving those events without which there would have been no Temple or pilgrimages to Zion.

What were the psalmist's words that carried so much weight historically, theologically and in "contemporizing" David's role related to pilgrims' worship?

Psalm 132

Remember, O Lord, on David's behalf,
All his affliction;
How he swore to the Lord,
And vowed to the Mighty One of Jacob,
"Surely I will not enter my house,
Nor lie on my bed;
I will not give sleep to my eyes,
Or slumber to my eyelids;
Until I find a place for the Lord,
A dwelling place for the Mighty One of Jacob."
Behold, we heard of it in Ephrathah;

We found it in the field of Jaar.
Let us go into His dwelling place;
Let us worship at His footstool.
Arise, O Lord, to Thy resting place;
Thou and the ark of Thy strength.
Let Thy priests be clothed with righteousness;
And let Thy godly ones sing for joy.
For the sake of David Thy servant,
Do not turn away the face of Thine anointed.
The Lord has sworn to David,
A truth from which He will not turn back;
"Of the fruit of your body I will set upon your throne.
If your sons will keep My covenant,
And My testimony which I will teach them,
Their sons shall also sit upon your throne forever."
For the Lord has chosen Zion;
He has desired it for His habitation.
"This is my resting place forever;
Here I will dwell, for I have desired it.
I will abundantly bless her provision;
I will satisfy her needy with bread.
Her priests also I will clothe with salvation;
And her godly ones will sing aloud for joy.
There I will cause the horn of David to spring forth;
I have prepared a lamp for Mine anointed.
His enemies I will clothe with shame;
But upon himself his crown shall shine."

(Ps. 132:1-18)

Obviously, there is a lot to digest here in Psalm 132. How did the psalmist "shape" his song in order to emphasize his major points?

A "Double-Take" on the Promises Related to David

Van Gemeren understands that Psalm 132 has a parallel structure that could be referred to as a "double-take." What I mean by that is, in Van Gemeren's understanding, the thought patterns of the first half of the psalm (vv. 1-9) are paralleled in the second half (vv. 10-18) by closely related ideas. It is almost as if you are looking at the same thing twice in rapid succession, i.e., a double-take.

As is seen in the following diagram, this makes for a beautifully symmetrical song:

A.   Prayer for David (v. 1)
B.   David's Devotion (vv. 2-5)
C.   David's Concern for God's Presence (vv. 6-9)
A'.   Prayer for David (v. 10)
B'.   God's Reward to David (vv. 11-12)
C'.   God's Presence in Zion (vv. 13-18) [1]

This structural outline does indeed have much to commend it. But it is unnecessarily vague at points. That is particularly true in verses 13-18, which seem to include a lot of detail that more than coincidentally, in smaller segments, parallels the earlier part of the psalm. I think it should be said that Van Gemeren's above outline is at least as much of a step forward in structural understanding as the difference between color and black and white television. However, as will be seen through the remainder of the discussion in this chapter, the following structure is more accurate to the actual parallelism of the psalm:

A. David swears to seek a dwelling place for the Lord (vv. 1-5)

B. Taking the ark up to Jerusalem, then going up to worship (vv. 6-8)

C. A request for priestly righteousness and joy for the godly (v. 9)

D. The Lord swears that David's descendants, if obedient, will sit on his throne forever (vv. 10-12)

A'. The Lord choosing Zion for His dwelling place (vv. 13-14)

B'. The Lord's abundant provision for Zion and her occupants (v. 15)

C'. A promise of salvation for the priests and joy for the godly (v. 16)

D'. The Lord will cause David and his line to prosper (vv. 17-18)

Seeking and Finding the Lord's Dwelling Place

The first set of parallels in Psalm 132 has to do with David swearing that he will not rest until he finds a dwelling place for the Lord, balanced by the Lord's choice of Zion as his eternal habitation. The initial section (vv. 1-5) embodies David's zeal to build the Temple, a similar passion to that expected in the Lord's pilgrims coming up to the feasts. The Lord responds to David's zealous oath with his emphatic decision that Zion will always be His dwelling place (vv. 13-14), which means He may still be found in "Zion" by those seeking Him.

Though there is no Temple on Mount Zion in Jerusalem today, His presence is, if anything, even more readily available. Both the individual bodies of Christians

(1 Cor. 6:19) and the corporate body of Christ, the church (1 Cor. 3:16) are the "temple" of the Holy Spirit under the New Covenant. He now dwells in and among His people at least as much as He did in the Temple in Jerusalem (Ps. 132:13-14). The first part of this pair (vv. 6-8) first relives how the ark was located, then taken to Jerusalem, where the Temple could be built to serve as the Lord's "footstool" and "resting place," but also where He could be worshiped.

It is shocking to remember that the ark of the covenant, having been returned by the Philistines who were cursed by its presence, stayed in Kiriath-Jearim (called "the field of Jaar" in verse 6) for almost a generation (see 1 Sam. 7; 2 Sam. 6). Given that the tablets of the Ten Commandments were inside the ark of the covenant, and that the ark represented the presence of God among His people, virtually "losing" the ark for that prolonged period indicates how incredibly insensitive the people were to the Lord and His Word, including His gracious promises.

Suffice it to say that David and those with him who brought up the ark to Jerusalem, then those who built the Temple, did their part. Then, as reflected by the wording in verse 15, the Lord more than held up His end of the bargain. The Lord promised to bless the provision for the Temple and her workers, as well as meet the needs for food by the poor who lived in the area around the Temple.

It is quite possible that Psalm 132:15 provides the biblical principle that is the basis for Philippians 4:19: "And my God shall supply all your needs according to His riches in glory in Christ Jesus." In that context, it must be understood that Paul is not making a blanket promise to just anyone or even every Christian. Rather, he is saying, in light of the Philippians' generous meeting of Paul's needs (Phil. 4:15-18), the Lord committed His matchless resources to meet their needs. By application, it is those today who invest themselves and their resources to meet others' needs, to whom the Lord promises that He will see that their needs will be met. What a promise for the Lord's children to meditate upon!

Verses 9 and 16 of Psalm 132 are so close in wording that it must be wondered whether they were originally sung as a short refrain or chorus. However, that should not in any sense be taken as implying that these verses are merely repetitive wording, much less "vain repetition." Rather, they made very important complementary points to the original pilgrims going up to the feasts in Jerusalem and continue to do so with equal force in the lives of God's pilgrims today.

Verse 9 voices a heartfelt request by the psalmist for two important spiritual "gifts." Now, by referring to such here, I am not talking about the gifts for service in the Body of Christ, as are discussed in Romans 12, 1 Corinthians 12 and 1 Peter 4. Rather, I am using the terminology in a more general sense: as gifts God gives that are spiritual in nature, having to do more generally with the ministry of the Holy Spirit.

The first part of the request is: "Let the priests be clothed with righteousness." The priests, of course, were the mediators, through the sacrificial system, between God and man under the Old Covenant. The reason sacrificial blood had to be shed was that "There is none righteous, not even one" (Rom. 3:10, citing Pss. 14 and 53). Therefore, the only way they could "be clothed with righteousness" was through the shedding of blood.

The answer to the first part of the request in Psalm 132:9 is voiced by the Lord in verse 16 in this way: "Her priests also I will clothe with salvation." Thus, the sacrifices being offered in the context of the Temple worship and, in the context of the Songs of Ascent, especially the sacrifices related to the great feasts, were indeed accomplishing their purpose. However, for the Old Testament pilgrim, the righteousness and salvation available through the priesthood was always a temporary reality. The sacrifices had to go on and on, because, "without the shedding of blood, there is no remission of sin."

For pilgrims under the New Covenant, though, there are three major changes:

1) Jesus Christ, "the Lamb of God who takes away the sins of the world," has offered a once-for-all sacrifice; 2) He is now our great High Priest, eternally; and 3) we are each believer-priests, permanently clothed in Christ's righteousness and salvation. Large chunks of the New Testament, notably in Romans and Hebrews, are given over to describing these blessings in the lives of believers today. That means, in looking at Psalm 132:16, we take part in the wider fulfillment of the wonderful promise of the first part of this verse today.

But, there is more here for us in the pairing in Psalm 132:9 and 16. Verse 9 beseeches: "And let the godly ones sing for joy." Verse 16 promises: "And her godly ones will sing aloud for joy." Who are these "godly ones?" Initially, this seems confusing, since "There is none righteous, not even one." The answer is in the Hebrew word that is used here. It is a cousin term to *hesed,* a primary Old Testament term for the Lord's gracious "loving-kindness." Thus, the focus in regard to these "godly ones," these Old Testament saints, is not their own godliness, but God's gracious provision for them of righteousness and salvation, even as He had done in regard to the priests. As a result, they certainly had every reason to "sing for joy."

Believers today are also "godly ones" (i.e., saints) strictly and only because of God's gracious provision in our Lord Jesus Christ. As such, we should also "sing aloud for joy," including the psalms, as evidence of the Spirit's filling of our lives (Eph. 5:18-20) and the spiritual fruit He is bringing about through us (Gal. 5:22-23). There is another major point of difference here between the Old Covenant pilgrim and those on a pilgrimage to draw closer to the Lord today, though. In Psalm 132, singing aloud for joy is mentioned in the context of going to Jerusalem and the Temple periodically for the worship of the feasts. New Covenant pilgrims, instead, are commanded to "Rejoice always" (1 Thess. 5:16). It is not to be just at Christian holidays, or at worship services or on the Lord's Day. Rather, every moment of every day is not just an opportunity, but an imperative responsibility before the Lord to express our joy in Him.

He Remembers David and the Promises... Do We?

God's covenant with David (see 2 Sam. 7:12-16) was indeed eternal ("forever" [Ps. 132:12]) in one sense. However, it was also conditional in another sense: "If your sons will keep My covenant" (v. 12). Sadly, that "if" was not something that King David's descendants could live up to. Though there were good kings, the predominance of wicked Davidic rulers eventually brought the Lord's judgment on the kingdom. Since the Babylonian Exile, there has been no descendant of David who has sat on a physical "throne" (Ps. 132:11, 12) in Israel.

That does not at all mean the Lord has not stood by His Word, though. The Lord has kept the promise He swore to David (Ps. 132:11): Jesus is the ultimate "son of David" (Matt. 1:1). In Jesus, the Lord's promise concerning "the horn of David," an even more powerful future ruler, who will achieve all that God has promised, is fulfilled.[2] He is the ultimate "Anointed One" in David's line (Ps. 132:10, 17). When "every knee shall bow... and every tongue confess that Jesus is Lord" at the end of the age (Phil. 2:10, 11), His enemies will be "clothed with shame" (Ps. 132:18).

With all this in mind, it cannot seriously be argued that the Lord has not remembered David and His great promises to him (Ps. 132). So, the attention now turns to us as the Lord's pilgrims. How consistently have we remembered God's promises? How much do we reflect, on a daily basis, on all the Lord has done for us, especially in and through the greatest Son of David: the Lord Jesus?

If the answer to those questions is, as it is for most of us, deep conviction of our inconsistency, just remember that is why we are talking about that now. We have arrived at Psalm 132. It is reminding us, calling us to re-enactment, calling us to closeness to the Lord who has made available to us the joy of our salvation. There is a line from an old Disney song that has stuck in my mind all through the years since I was a small child: "Whistle while you work." The general idea is that, if you whistle as you are engaged in your labor, things will be noticeably more pleasant. That is probably true more often than not. However, the question that I think should be asked is: "Other than a subjective emotional lift, what else is gained when you whistle while you work?" The honest answer would have to be, "Not much, other than killing time."

By contrast, when the Christian chooses to meditate on God's Word while he or she is moving ahead on the pilgrimage the Lord asks to be undertaken, wonderful spiritual stability is developed and marvelous dividends are earned, even in this life:

> How blessed is the man
> who does not walk in the counsel of the wicked,
> Nor stand in the path of sinners,
> Nor sit in the seat of scoffers.
> But his delight is in the law of the Lord,
> And in His law he meditates day and night

And he will be like a tree firmly planted by streams of waters,
Which yields its fruit in its season,
And its leaf does not wither;
And in whatever he does, he prospers.

(Ps. 1:1-3)

The Lord's pilgrim consistently meditates on God's promises of salvation. The Lord delights in those who do this. He faithfully and consistently fulfills his word; therefore, the Lord's pilgrims gain strength and confidence as they meditate on his works.

Notes

[1] Willem Van Gemeren, "Psalms," in the *Expositor's Bible Commentary*, Vol. 5; Gen. Ed. Frank E. Gaebelein (Grand Rapids: Zondervan, 1991)

[2] James M. Boice, *Psalms: An Expositional Commentary*, Vol. 3 (Grand Rapids: Baker, 1998) p. 1151.

SEVEN

~~~~~~

"Praise the Lord!"
The Worshiping Life: Psalms 133-134

The "Wind" in the Congregation: Breath of Fresh Air, Dry as Dust or Icy Gust?

While I make no claim to special spiritual insight, I have noticed three types of prevailing "wind/weather patterns" that blow through most, if not all, local churches. Now, with some congregations, things may be more subtle and the diagnosis may take a little longer. But, in most cases, attending just a handful of worship services — often only one or two — is sufficient to give you the "feel" of which of these three general types you are looking at.

First, you often hear people lament that this church is "dead." That, of course, is entirely possible, if the Reformation gospel of salvation by grace through faith (Eph. 2:8-9) has not been preached in that congregation. In that case, those in attendance would still be spiritually "dead in their trespasses and sins" (Eph. 2:1). However, in situations in which the congregation is, instead, made up of believers, what is often referred to as "deadness" is perhaps more accurately termed "dry and exhausting." Instead of being invigorated by attending the worship, you leave either lethargic or feeling spiritually drained. It's like having to contend with a hot, dry wind: something in the air is moving, yes; but it provides no relief. It gradually drains the sweat out of you and leaves you like a limp dishrag. If there is a church in Scripture that is significantly similar to this, it would be the church at Laodicea, which, though going through the motions fairly impressively, is severly warned by the Lord for having a lukewarm attitude (Rev. 3:14-22). The second common "feel" I have in many churches is the chilling blast. Now, by that, I do not primarily mean that they are unfriendly to visitors. Rather, it has to do with how they relate to each other. Like Euodia and Syntyche in the church at Philippi (Phil. 4:2-3), who were seriously at odds with one another, feuding believers — and, make no mistake, a "cold war" can be just as painful as an open dispute — can cause the "warmth" of the fellowship and worship of a congregation to plummet precipitously.

Fortunately, there are also churches in which the worship is "a breath of fresh air" and it is spiritually encouraging and invigorating. What makes the difference? It is that "the unity of the Spirit, in the bond of peace" (Eph. 4:3) is on display. In obedience to what the Lord Jesus singled out as the two greatest commandments in the entire Mosaic Law (Matt. 22:34-40), these people really love the Lord and each other. And it makes a dramatic difference – a very winsome difference, I might add – in the looks on the faces of the individual worshipers, as well as the underlying tone of the worship service.

The Consecrating Refreshment of Unity

This last category of worship is what is envisioned and beautifully pictured in Psalm 133. Though it is one of the shortest of the Psalms of Ascent, its importance should not be underestimated. As Anglican bishop Stewart Perowne insightfully put it in the nineteenth century:

> Nowhere has the nature of true unity – that unity that binds men together, not by artificial restraints, but as brethren of one heart – been more faithfully described, nowhere has it been so gracefully illustrated, as in this short ode.[1]

And, for the weary pilgrims soon to arrive in Jerusalem for the feast, and about to renew relationships with family members, this was a pointed, but hopeful, reminder. The time that they would spend together in worship and interacting with others had the wonderful potential of much more than just going through the motions and logging time.

> Behold, how good and how pleasant it is
> For brothers to dwell together in unity.
> It is like the precious oil upon the head,
> Coming down upon the beard,
> Even Aaron's beard,
> Coming down upon the edge of his robes.
> It is like the dew of Hermon,
> Coming down upon the mountains of Zion;
> For there the Lord commanded the blessing—life forever.
>
> (Ps. 133:1-3)

As will be seen, the theme of Psalm 133 is, clearly, the unity of the brethren, which is lauded and vividly described. However, as we begin this discussion of the next-to-last of the pilgrim psalms, we must not forget the context we have considered every step along the way in the pilgrim's journey. The purpose of the pilgrimage in going up to Jerusalem was worship in relation to the Temple. However, for that worship to be everything the Lord intended, both for this life and eternity, a profound oneness in both horizontal and vertical relationships needed to be forged.

In looking at the structure of Psalm 133, once again Van Gemeren has displayed real insight in detecting its inverted parallel structure:

A.   Blessing (v. 1)
B.   Comparison with Oil (v. 2a)

C.   Aaronic Ministry (v. 2b)
B'. Comparison with Dew (v. 3a)
A'. Blessing (v. 3a)[2]

Though many experts have not noted such a structure, the "blessing" angles at the beginning and end of the psalm (vv. 1, 3b), without question, are paired by the author. Just as obvious is the clearly parallel wording of the analogies of the oil and the dew (vv. 2, 3a). The following outline is essentially the same as Van Gemeren's. The only other difference is that I have attempted to provide enough nuance in the wording of each section of the outline to make it clear how each relates to the overall theme of unity against the historical context of the pilgrims' worship.

A.   The blessing of brethren dwelling together in unity in the context of worship (v. 1)
B.   The analogy of unity to the sanctifying anointing with oil, coming down on the high priest, the leader of worship (v. 2)
B'. The analogy of unity to the refreshing dew of Hermon, coming down on the place
of worship in Zion (v. 3a)
A'. The blessing of life forever and together, related to unity of worship in Zion (v. 3b)

The eye-catching aspect of the two parallel similes is the repeated wording "coming down on" (vv. 2, 3a). The imagery of both is very rich, calling to mind the sense of the Lord's extravagant blessings descending on his people. And, as we will see in the discussions below, both analogies have great meaning in the context of the pilgrim's journey.

David's Perspective on "Family" Unity

The superscription of Psalm 133 attributes its authorship to David. While that is by no means certain, there is no compelling reason to deny that David wrote the psalm, either. If David is indeed the author, there is intriguing background to consider in his choice of the theme of "brotherly unity" for the psalm. For example, when he was young, his own family did not exactly rally around him when he was anointed by Samuel to be king (1 Sam. 16) or when he stepped forward to fight Goliath (1 Sam. 17). Then, he watched the deep and bitter division in King Saul's family over David's friendship with Jonathan, Saul's eldest son. Finally, on the largest scale, it was seven and a half years before David could heal the deep division and unite all twelve tribes under his rulership as king (2 Sam. 5:1-5).

Thus, given his broad painful experience with brotherly disunity, it seems that there are few people who could appreciate how "good" and "pleasant" family unity truly is any more than David. Surely that must be a large part of the reason why he seems to value and prioritize the unity of the brethren to the degree that he does. Of course, this beautiful description of brotherly unity is sketched against the backdrop of the pilgrims arriving in Jerusalem for one of the feasts and staying at least several days in very close quarters. It must not be forgotten, either, that when David wrote the psalm, the city of

Jerusalem had only recently been taken by Israel from the Jebusites (2 Sam. 5) and, at the time, was not large either geographically or population-wise. Thus, from the very beginning of the pilgrimages to Jerusalem, there would have been very close fellowship, so to speak.

Over time, the city grew and with the population of Israel, the number of pilgrims going up to the feasts grew dramatically. During the New Testament era, the greatly-enlarged city of Jerusalem is seen packed to the gills with pilgrims for the Feast of Pentecost in Acts 2. All of this is to make a very practical point: when people are crowded, especially for any period of time, it is not easy to get along. The achieving and maintaining of unity is made just that much more difficult. But, it is doable, and, as we shall see, especially for God's pilgrims living under the New Covenant.

The Consecrating Effect of Family Unity

A natural tendency in Psalm 133:2 may be to focus on the high priest. But the spotlight here is definitely on the "oil" used to anoint the priest and on its effect on the priest who has been anointed. The oil was of a unique blend directed by the Lord (Ex. 30:22-33). It had a very specific, and critical, purpose before the Lord, which was not to be compromised:

> And you shall anoint Aaron and his sons, and consecrate them, that they minister as priests to me. And you shall speak to the sons of Israel, saying, "This shall be a holy anointing oil to Me throughout your generations.

It shall not be poured on anyone's body, nor shall you
make any like it, in the same proportion; it is holy, and
it shall be holy to you. Whoever shall mix any like it, or
whoever puts any of it on a layman, shall be cut off from
his people" (Ex. 30:30-33).

Thus, you could almost say that the anointing oil for the
priest virtually "took on a life of its own" for the people
of Israel. Most likely, what is envisioned in Psalm 133:2
is a scene similar to Leviticus 8:30, in which Aaron and
his sons were anointed in the presence of the entire
"congregation" of the people there in the Wilderness
(Lev. 8:3-4). When the anointing oil was poured over
Aaron's head, then dripped down over his beard and
vestments, he was consecrated for ministry unto the Lord,
a joyful occasion for all the people.

And that seems to be the picture that David wants to
compare and apply in regard to the unity of the brethren
(Ps. 133:1). We can state the comparison this way: the
unity of the brethren is good and pleasant because it
consecrates the brethren for ministry before the Lord. In
that regard, the "trickle-down effect" of the oil may be
meant to imply that, just as the oil eventually covered all
parts of Aaron's body, so all of the unified brethren (v. 1)
are consecrated and expected to minister.

This is a very important point for each pilgrim to
understand. Each believer is intended to be consecrated, to
be set apart in holiness, to worship and minister unto the
Lord. Even though not all are called to formal ministry,
all are consecrated to some kind of ministry unto Him.

But the crucial implication of the linkage of verses 1 and 2 is that it is only in the context of the unity of the brethren when that consecration is poured out.

What that means for our pilgrimage is that it may be necessary for us to seek to repair relationships within our congregation. We may have to swallow some pride and self-centeredness in doing so (Phil. 2:3-4). But, the dividends are incredible: 1) good and pleasant unity among the brethren; and 2) consecration to ministry for the whole congregation. And, we haven't even explored the pay-off in verse 3 yet.

Mount Zion is hot and dry for most of the year, including the seasons of two of the feasts (Pentecost, in the early Summer; and Tabernacles, in the early Fall). Mount Hermon, in stark contrast, is always cool and well-watered. So, the coolness and supply of water is transferred from Hermon to Zion, being pictured as a refreshing dew descending on the Temple and the Holy City. What a beautiful dimension of unity this describes. It is "good and pleasant" to be with the brethren because it is refreshing.

And what a difference that makes in our attitudes. To be able to go to church, or any other meeting of Christians, and then to go home or to any other responsibility or activity invigorated and encouraged, instead of worn out and discouraged, is a phenomenal blessing. If nothing else, attendance and participation goes up significantly just because the members love being together instead of feeling like they are going to a dentist's appointment.

For the pilgrim seeking to journey closer, into God's presence, this is a very important factor, also. Not only is there a need to be consecrated to worship (the First Commandment: "Love the Lord") and ministry on the journey, but because it is a long, hard climb, the need for refreshment and encouragement is frequent. And, much of that refreshing and encouraging is provided, one pilgrim to another, as we fulfill the Second Commandment by loving our neighbors and bearing one another's burdens along the way as we draw ever closer to our destination.

It is not immediately clear what David means when he concludes Psalm 133 with "For there the Lord commanded the blessing – life forever." At first glance, since the closest antecedent to "there" is "the mountains of Zion," in the earlier part of verse 3, it appears that "life evermore" must have something to do with the Temple worship. Or, perhaps it is the work of Christ that is pictured in the sacrifices, which will be the basis for eternal life under the New Covenant.

But it can also refer back to the overarching theme of the psalm: the unity of the brethren. If that is the case, the point of the wording at the end of the psalm is to pick up and extend the parallel idea in verse 1. Life together as brethren, which, when unified, is good and pleasant (v. 1), consecrated and refreshing (vv. 2-3a), here and now, is intended to be a permanent, not a temporary, state. This involves worship, because, as we will discuss in the next section, that is a much broader concept than in the Old Testament, even much broader than most of us assume.

True Worshipers: In Spirit and Truth… and Unity: Psalm 134

In John 4, when the woman at the well sought to sidetrack Jesus into the ongoing dispute between the Jews and the Samaritans over the correct place to worship (i.e., in Jerusalem, according to the Jews; at Mt Gerizim, according to the Samaritans), the Lord countered with:

> Woman, believe Me, an hour is coming when neither in this mountain, nor in Jerusalem, shall you worship the Father. … But an hour is coming, and now is, when the true worshipers shall worship the Father in spirit and truth; for such people the Father seeks to be His worshipers. God is spirit, and those who worship Him must worship in spirit and truth (John 4:21, 23-24).

There is much here that those on the pilgrim journey today need to understand about worship. Since Jesus brought in the New Covenant through the once-for-all sacrifice of His death on the Cross, and then the promised Spirit came to indwell and empower believers after Pentecost (John 14:17; Acts 2), things have changed remarkably in regard to many aspects of worship.

Under the Old Covenant, when the pilgrims were originally singing the Songs of Ascent as they went up to Jerusalem for the feasts, the place, timing and form of worship were all paramount considerations. It was necessary to go to the Temple, to be there on the days set apart for the particular feast and to give the appropriate sacrifice in the correct manner. Otherwise, proper worship had not taken place. This is evident in Psalm 134.

For New Covenant pilgrims, the only two bottom-line priorities are worshiping "in spirit" and "in truth." [3] And, amazingly enough, while the issues of when, where and how to worship still rear their heads frequently, often causing heated theological and practical ministry debates, relatively little is usually heard about Jesus' definitive perspective: "True worshipers shall worship the father in spirit and in truth... Those who worship Him must worship in spirit and truth." In other words, the other issues of worship with which congregations are often virtually obsessed pale to the point of utter meaninglessness unless the worship is "in spirit and in truth."

What do those two brief, but profound, phrases mean? To worship "in spirit" means at least that "the heart of worship" is the heart, the unseen spiritual part of mankind. How we "worship" on the outside begins with our spiritual state on the inside.

Simply focusing on getting the motions of "worship" right on the outside is little, if any, different from the "white-washed tomb" religion Jesus condemned in Matthew 23.

Worshiping "in spirit" may also refer (i.e., in a "both/and" manner) to worshiping in the power of the Holy Spirit. Ephesians 5:19-20 is certainly a worship context that follows hard on the heels of the command to "be filled with the Spirit" in 5:18. That also makes sense given how significant the Holy Spirit and His ministry is in the Gospel of John, in which particular emphasis is given to looking forward to the Spirit's ministry in Jesus' physical absence, after the Ascension (see especially John 14-16, the

Upper Room Discourse). Worshiping "in truth" must also be considered in its context in the Fourth Gospel. Toward the end, Pontius Pilate asks the philosophically loaded question: "What is truth?" (John 18:38). Fortunately, the question had already been answered in some depth earlier in the Gospel. "I am the way, the truth and the life," said Jesus in John 14:6 and He is said to be full of "grace and truth" in 1:14. He also asserted: "Thy Word is truth," speaking of the Scriptures, in His great high priestly prayer (John 17:17). And, in an interesting link to the phrase "in spirit," the Holy Spirit is repeatedly referred to as "the Spirit of truth" (John 14:17; 15:26; 16:13).

Thus, in summary, as we prepare to come to the climax of our pilgrim journey, it seems fair to say that worshiping "in spirit and truth" includes the following elements:

1) worshiping with a heart that is right before the Lord; 2) worshiping in the power of the Holy Spirit; 3) worship that centers on, and glorifies, Jesus Christ, who is the living Word of truth; and 4) worship that is in accord with the Bible, the written Word of truth.

When those scriptural priorities for worship are carried out, and there is unity with the brethren, the two Great Commandments are being fulfilled, and the Lord's pilgrim can know that the road ahead in the pilgrimage, no matter how difficult, will be worshipful and blessed.

Notes

[1] J. J. Stewart Perowne, as cited by James M. Boice, in "Psalms:" *An Expositional Commentary*, Vol. 3 (Grand Rapids: Baker, 1998) p. 1159.

[2] Willem Van Gemeren, "Psalms," in the *Expositor's Bible Commentary*, Vol. 5; Gen. Ed. Frank E. Gaebelein (Grand Rapids: Zondervan, 1991) p. 815.

[3] In discussing worship here, I have picked up, and further developed, a crucial topic for Christian living that I initially probed in A. Boyd Luter, "Worship as Service: The New Testament Usage of *Latreuo*," *Criswell Theological Review*, 1988.

CONCLUSION

~~~~~~~~~~~~~~~~~~~~~~~~~~~~~~

The Journey's End

The first question of the Westminster
Shorter Catechism is this: *What is the
chief end of man?* Answer: *Man's chief
end is to glorify God, and to enjoy Him forever.*
As I have tried to demonstrate, the pilgrim
psalms present us with a reliable process
to reach that end. The journey begins with
an understanding that this world is not
our home. Thus, the pilgrimage is sought
when discontentment with the world sets
in (Ps. 120).

Godly dependence is the next step. To admit helplessness and utter dependence on God's mercy actually catapults us "up the hills." Those who trust in the Lord at this point are as solid as a rock and are able to make the rest of the journey in his strength (Pss. 125-129). Once godly dependence characterizes our daily lives, we are in a place to behold the glory of God in a deeper way. We begin to acknowledge that true blessings, both physical and spiritual, come from Him. The closer we are to the Temple, the more we acknowledge and embrace this reality (Pss. 126-129).

The closer we move to the inner courts of the Temple, the more we become aware of our sin. Therefore, confession and humility are the necessary next steps in the journey. The Lord is the only one who can forgive sin; therefore, He is to be greatly feared (Pss. 130-131). In this humble state, in this waiting mode, the Lord's pilgrim is given the opportunity to meditate on His many promises of salvation. The Lord delights in those who meditate on his word. Because He faithfully and consistently fulfills his word, the Lord's pilgrims gain strength and confidence as they meditate on his works (Ps. 132).

The Lord's mature pilgrims, the ones who have followed the way of discipline and have taken this glorious journey, will dwell in the inner courts of the Temple in Zion in consistent unity with the "assembly." The Lord's blessings flow from Zion, and these blessings make unity possible (Pss. 133-134). In this setting is fulfilled the two greatest commandments: Love the Lord your God with all your heart and your neighbor as yourself. Thus, we are brought to our final end: to glorify God and enjoy Him forever!

Our Glorious End: Down through the Centuries

I hope to have encouraged you to take this upward journey into the Lord's presence. It is my hope that you will read Psalms 120-134 frequently and prayerfully. It is also my fervent prayer that you will "enlarge your soul" by reading about some of the spiritual journeys of saints throughout church history. We have such a rich spiritual heritage here in the West, and, unfortunately, it has been forgotten by most of us. I have been so blessed by the spiritual pilgrimages of some of the devout believers of the Christian tradition that I want to leave you with samples of the way in which some of them visualized our final end:

Psalm 134

Praise the Lord,
all you servants of the Lord
who minster by night in the
house of the Lord.
Lift up your hands in the
sanctuary
and praise the Lord.
May the Lord, the Maker of
heaven and earth,
bless you from Zion.

Augustine – *Confessions*

Late have I loved you, beauty so old and so new: late have I loved you. And see, you were within and I was in the external world and sought you there, and in my unlovely state I plunged into those lovely created things which you made. You were with me, and I was not with you. The lovely things kept me far from you, though if they did not have their existence in you, they had no existence at all. You called and cried out loud and shattered my deafness. You were radiant and resplendent, you put to flight my blindness. You were fragrant, and I drew in my breath and now pant after you. I tasted you, and I feel but hunger and thirst for you. You touched me, and I am set on fire to attain the peace which is yours.[1]

Anselm – *Proslogion*

My God and my Lord, my hope and the joy of my heart, tell my soul if this is the joy of which You speak through Your Son: 'Ask and you will receive, that your joy may be complete' [John 16:24]. For I have discovered a joy that is complete and more than complete. Indeed, when the heart is filled with that joy, the mind is filled with it, the soul is filled with it, the whole man is filled with it, yet joy beyond measure will remain. The whole of that joy, then, will not enter into those who rejoice, but those who rejoice will enter wholly into that joy. Speak, Lord, tell Your servant within his heart if this is the joy into which Your servants will enter who enter 'into the joy of the Lord' [Matt. 25:21]. But surely that joy in which Your chosen ones will rejoice is that which 'neither eye has seen, nor ear heard, nor has it entered into the heart of man' [1 Cor. 2:9]. I have not yet said or thought, then, Lord, how greatly your blessed will rejoice. They will, no doubt, rejoice as much as they love, and they will love as much as they know. How much will they know You, then, Lord, and how much will they love You? In very truth, 'neither eye has seen, nor ear heard, nor has it entered into the heart of man' [ibid] in this life how much they will know You and love You in that life.

I pray, O God, that I may know You and love You, so that I may rejoice in You. And if I cannot do so fully in this life may I progress gradually until it comes to fullness. Let the knowledge of You grow in me here, and there [in heaven] be made complete; let Your love grow in me here and there be made complete, so that here my joy may be great in hope, and there be complete in reality. Lord, by Your Son You command, or rather, counsel us to ask and you promise that we shall receive so that our 'joy may be complete' [John 16:24]. I ask, Lord, as You counsel through our admirable counsellor. May I receive what You promise through Your truth so that my 'joy may be complete' [ibid]. Until then let my mind meditate on it, let my tongue speak of it, let my heart love it, let my mouth preach it. Let my soul hunger for it, let my flesh thirst for it, my whole being desire it, until I enter into the 'joy of the Lord' [Matt. 25:21], who is God, Three in One, 'blessed forever. Amen' [Rom. 1:25].[2]

Bonaventure — *The Soul's Journey Into God*

But you, my friend,
concerning mystical visions,
with your journey more firmly determined,
leave behind
your senses and intellectual activities,
sensible and invisible things,
all nonbeing and being;
and in this state of unknowing
be restored,
insofar as is possible,
to unity with him
who is above all essence and knowledge.
For transcending yourself and all things,
by the immeasurable and absolute ecstasy of a pure mind,
leaving behind all things
and freed from all things,
you will ascend
to the superessential ray
of the divine darkness.

But if you wish to know how these things come about,
ask grace not instruction,
desire not understanding,
the groaning of prayer not diligent reading,
the Spouse not the teacher,
God not man,
darkness not clarity,
not light but the fire
that totally inflames and carries us into God
by ecstatic unctions and burning affections.

This fire is God,
and his furnace is in Jerusalem;
and Christ enkindles it
in the heat of his burning passion,
which only he truly perceives who says:
My soul chooses hanging and my bones death.

Whoever loves this death
can see God
because it is true beyond doubt that
"man will not see me and live."
Let us, then, die
and enter into the darkness;
let us impose silence
upon our cares, our desires and our imaginings.
With Christ crucified
let us pass out of this world to the Father
so that when the Father is shown to us,
we may say with Philip:
"It is enough for us."
Let us hear with Paul:
"My grace is sufficient for you."
Let us rejoice with David saying:
"My flesh and my heart have grown faint;
You are the God of my heart,
and the God that is my portion forever.
Blessed be the Lord forever
and all the people will say:
Let it be; let it be.
Amen."

Here Ends the Soul's Journey into God[3]

Dante – *Paradise*

And so my mind, bedazzled and amazed,
Stood fixed in wonder, motionless, intent,
And still my wonder kindled as I gazed.

That light doth so transform a man's [or mind's?]
whole bent
That never to another sight or thought
Would he surrender, with his own consent;

For everything the will has ever sought
Is gathered there, and there is every quest
Made perfect, which apart from it falls short.

Now, that the living light I looked on wore
More semblances than one, which cannot be,
For it is always what it was before;

But as my sight by seeing learned to see,
The transformation which in me took place
Transformed the single changeless form for me.

That light supreme, within its fathomless
Clear substance, showed to me three spheres, which
bare
Three hues distinct, and occupied one space;

The first mirrored the next, as though it were
Rainbow from rainbow, and the third seemed flame
Breathed equally from each of the first pair.

How weak are words, and how unfit to frame
My concept — which lags after what was shown
So far, twould flatter it to call it lame!

Eternal light, that in Thyself alone
Dwelling, alone dost know Thyself, and smile
On Thy self-love, so knowing and so known!

The sphering thus begot, perceptible
In Thee like mirrored light, now to my view —
When I had looked on it a little while —

Seemed in itself, and in its own self-hue,
Limned with our image; for which cause mine eyes
Were altogether drawn and held thereto.

As the geometer his mind applies
To square the circle, not for all his wit
Finds the right formula, however he tries,

So strove I with that wonder — how to fit
The image to the sphere; so sought to see
How it maintained the point of rest in it.

Thither my own wings could not carry me,
But that a flash my understanding clove,
Whence its desire came to it suddenly.

High phantasy lost power and here broke off;
Yet, as a wheel moves smoothly, free from jars,
My will and my desire were turned to love,

The love that moves the sun and the other stars.[4]

John Bunyan – *Pilgrim's Progress*

Now, when they were come up to the gate, there was written over it in letters of gold, "Blessed are they that do his commandments, that they may have right to the tree of life, and may enter in through the gates into the city" (Rev. 22:14). ...

These pilgrims are come from the city of Destruction, for the love that they bear to the King of this place. Then the pilgrims give in unto them each man his certificate, which they had received in the beginning. Those therefore were carried in to the King, who read them. ...

Now, just as the gates were opened to let in the men, I looked in after them, and behold the City shone like the sun; the streets also were paved with gold; and in them walked many men, with crowns on their heads, palms in their hands, and golden harps, to sing praises withal.

There were also of them that had wings, and they answered one another without intermission saying: Holy, holy, holy, is the Lord! And after that they shut up the gates. ...[5]

John Henry Newman – *The Preaching of John Henry Newman*

May it be our blessedness, as years go on, to add one grace to another, and advance upward, step by step, neither neglecting the lower after attaining the higher, not aiming at the higher before attaining the lower. The first grace is faith, the last is love; first comes zeal, afterwards comes loving-kindness; first comes humiliation, then comes peace; first comes diligence, then comes resignation. May we learn to mature all graces in us; fearing and trembling, watching and repenting, because Christ is coming; joyful, thankful, and careless of the future, because he is come.[6]

Notes

[1]Augustine, *Confessions*, p. 201.

[2]Anselm, *Proslogion*, pp.103-104.

[3]Bonaventure, *The Soul's Journey into God*, *The Tree of Life*, *The Life of Francis*, trans. by Ewert Cousins (New York: Paulist Press, 1978), pp. 114-116.

[4]Dante, *Paradise*, trans. by Dorothy Sayers and Barbara Reynolds, (New York: Penguin Books, 1962), pp. 346-347.

[5]John Bunyan, *Pilgrim's Progress*, (Chicago: Moody Press, 1989), pp. 188-189.

[6]John Henry Newman, *The Preaching of John Henry Newman*, ed. W.E. White (Philadelphia: Fortress Press, 1969), pp. 211.

Finding the Life You're Longing for from Psalm 23
SONG OF A SATISFIED SOUL
JOHN A. KITCHEN
'The ideal book to share with those needing encouragement.'
Warren W. Wiersbe
A • REAL • CHANGE • BOOK

Song of a Satisfied Soul
Finding the Life You're Longing for from Psalm 23
John A. Kitchen

'…beautifully sketches for us the one true source of true contentment. It will make the reader see a familiar passage of scripture from a fresh outlook. A must for anyone searching for true satisfaction and renewal in a world full of need.'

Rajendra Pillai

'Shot through with vivid illustrations and stories, *The Song of a Satisfied Soul* is going to end up at bedsides, in hip pockets, and handbags, and on preachers' desks.'

Richard Bewes

We all long for satisfaction. More often than not dashed hopes and frustrated efforts leave us wondering if it is a phantom appetite - forever defying fulfillment. Broken promises, shattered relationships, lost jobs, unfulfilled hopes, dreams and aspirations- they mock us over past failures and our inability to lay hold of the satisfaction we long for. No sooner do we achieve a major goal in life than another immediately presents itself – leaving us in a perpetual chase after contentment.

Above the jeers, however, there rises the sweet strains of a hopeful song. The voice is familiar. The words are well known. But the hope is fresh. The disarming melody melts away despair and disbelief, bidding us to sing along. It is the song of a satisfied soul rising from a contented heart.

In the 23rd Psalm God lifts before us the Song of the Satisfied Soul. It's the promise of a life better than you've dreamt possible. God offers us the intimacy of a personal relationship with Himself. God Himself is our song, the singer, and the substance of the *Song of the Satisfied Soul*.

True satisfaction in life is found not when all want is removed,
but when above all we want Christ.

John A. Kitchen is a Pastor from Ohio who has previously authored *Embracing Authority* (ISBN 1-85792-715-X) – a counter-cultural look at how Christians should view authority.

ISBN 1-85792-942-X

Meditations on the Sufficiency of God

A MIGHTY FORTRESS

T·M·MOORE

A·REAL·CHANGE·BOOK

A Mighty Fortress
Meditations on the Sufficiency of God
T M Moore

God writes a lyric through our life. Through the means of praise and worship we can express our spiritual yearnings in ways that we would find difficult in everyday words or conversation.

Yet lyrics to hymns and songs become dry on our tongues. What once seemed to express our joy with incandescence, now glows feebly. We move on to new songs, only for the pattern to repeat itself. Nothing seems to last.

The problem is not the song, the problem is OUR song.

Using the verses from the great hymn 'A Mighty Fortress is our God', written from Martin Luther's meditations on psalm 46, T. M. Moore helps us recapture our song, written by God's hand in our life.

Rekindle the flames of your spiritual life and have a firmer footing to face the future.

At trying times Luther would turn to his closest friend and say 'Come Philip*, let us sing the 46th.' May your life also be turned into a more joyful song by staying in harmony with the God of all Creation. * Philip Melancthon

T. M. Moore is a Fellow of the Wilberforce Forum and Pastor of Teaching Ministries at Cedar Springs Presbyterian Church in Knoxville, Tennessee. His essays, reviews, articles, and poetry have appeared in a wide range of journals, and he is the author of 10 books, including *Preparing the Church for Revival ISBN 1 85792 698 6*. He and his wife, Susie, have four children and ten grandchildren, and make their home in Concord, TN.

ISBN 1 85792 8687

WOMEN

AS CHRIST'S DISCIPLES

BOYD LUTER
KATHY MCREYNOLDS

MODELS IN THE NEW TESTAMENT CHURCH FOR COURAGEOUS WOMEN TODAY

Women as Christ's Disciples
Models in the New Testament church for courageous women today
Boyd Luter and Kathy McReynolds

When we think of New Testament disciples, it is not usually women who come to mind – but they should.

Women were amongst Christ's earliest disciples. They did not have a back seat in the development of the church and they did not behave like their surrounding culture expected.

The study of Christ's female disciples has been largely ignored by conservative scholars, the subject being left to those with liberal and feminist agendas. This is a timely corrective that takes the Bible as it's guide and world-view.

Boyd Luter and Kathy McReynolds use examples of women during Christ's ministry, and from the early church, to develop a pattern of discipleship for women today.

These first women disciples were strong and courageous - models for contemporary Christian women (and men).

A. Boyd Luter is Professor of Biblical and Theological Studies at the Criswell College. He has written many books including a Focus on the Bible Commentary on Ruth and Esther, *God Behind the Seen* (ISBN 1 85792 8059 – co-authored with Barry C. Davis). A father of three, he lives in Texas.

Kathy McReynolds is on the faculty of Biola University and has authored many books and has contributed several articles to *The Evangelical Dictionary of World Missions*.

ISBN 1 85792 859 8